ELEMENTS OF HUMAN RESOURCE MANAGEMENT

For

B.B.M. (Semester - II)

As Per Savitribai Phule Pune University's New Syllabus,

Effective from June 2013

Anamika Ghosh
MBA (Marketing & Personnel Management)
Pratibha College of Commerce and Computer Studies

Tanvi Pandit
Masters in Journalism and
Mass Communication

N2942

Elements of Human Resource Management ISBN 978-93-83750-37-5

Third Edition : June 2015
© : Authors

The text of this publication, or any part thereof, should not be reproduced or transmitted in any form or stored in any computer storage system or device for distribution including photocopy, recording, taping or information retrieval system or reproduced on any disc, tape, perforated media or other information storage device etc., without the written permission of Authors with whom the rights are reserved. Breach of this condition is liable for legal action.

Every effort has been made to avoid errors or omissions in this publication. In spite of this, errors may have crept in. Any mistake, error or discrepancy so noted and shall be brought to our notice shall be taken care of in the next edition. It is notified that neither the publisher nor the authors or seller shall be responsible for any damage or loss of action to any one, of any kind, in any manner, therefrom.

Published By :
NIRALI PRAKASHAN
Abhyudaya Pragati, 1312, Shivaji Nagar,
Off J.M. Road, PUNE – 411005
Tel - (020) 25512336/37/39, Fax - (020) 25511379
Email : niralipune@pragationline.com

Printed By :
Repro Knowledgecast Limited,
Thane

☞ DISTRIBUTION CENTRES

PUNE
Nirali Prakashan : 119, Budhwar Peth, Jogeshwari Mandir Lane, Pune 411002, Maharashtra
Tel : (020) 2445 2044, 66022708, Fax : (020) 2445 1538
Email : bookorder@pragationline.com, niralilocal@pragationline.com

Nirali Prakashan : S. No. 28/27, Dhyari, Near Pari Company, Pune 411041
Tel : (020) 24690204 Fax : (020) 24690316
Email : dhyari@pragationline.com, bookorder@pragationline.com

MUMBAI
Nirali Prakashan : 385, S.V.P. Road, Rasdhara Co-op. Hsg. Society Ltd.,
Girgaum, Mumbai 400004, Maharashtra
Tel : (022) 2385 6339 / 2386 9976, Fax : (022) 2386 9976
Email : niralimumbai@pragationline.com

☞ DISTRIBUTION BRANCHES

JALGAON
Nirali Prakashan : 34, V. V. Golani Market, Navi Peth, Jalgaon 425001,
Maharashtra, Tel : (0257) 222 0395, Mob : 94234 91860

KOLHAPUR
Nirali Prakashan : New Mahadvar Road, Kedar Plaza, 1st Floor Opp. IDBI Bank
Kolhapur 416 012, Maharashtra. Mob : 9850046155

NAGPUR
Pratibha Book Distributors : Above Maratha Mandir, Shop No. 3, First Floor,
Rani Jhanshi Square, Sitabuldi, Nagpur 440012, Maharashtra
Tel : (0712) 254 7129

DELHI
Nirali Prakashan : 4593/21, Basement, Aggarwal Lane 15, Ansari Road, Daryaganj
Near Times of India Building, New Delhi 110002
Mob : 08505972553

BENGALURU
Pragati Book House : House No. 1, Sanjeevappa Lane, Avenue Road Cross,
Opp. Rice Church, Bengaluru – 560002.
Tel : (080) 64513344, 64513355, Mob : 9880582331, 9845021552
Email:bharatsavla@yahoo.com

CHENNAI
Pragati Books : 9/1, Montieth Road, Behind Taas Mahal, Egmore,
Chennai 600008 Tamil Nadu, Tel : (044) 6518 3535,
Mob : 94440 01782 / 98450 21552 / 98805 82331,
Email : bharatsavla@yahoo.com

niralipune@pragationline.com | www.pragationline.com

Also find us on www.facebook.com/niralibooks

Preface ...

Human Resource Management is a process that is designed to enhance employee performance overall. Thus, it is a series of actions that are taken in order to achieve excellence in employee performance.

Good practices in Human Resources are essentially tools that allow companies to achieve their goals and to boost both efficiency and productivity. Several human resource management practices include Recruitment and Selection, Job Analysis and Design, Manpower Planning, Performance Management, Training and Development, Employee Relations and much more.

This book of **Elements of Human Resource Management** covers the essentials of HRM as prescribed in the new revised syllabus by the Savitribai Phule Pune University for **BBM Semester II.**

With more and more people working for international corporations or global international supply chains, the study of international human resources is becoming ever more important. International Human Resource Management has therefore been included in the syllabus.

Being familiar with the needs of the teachers and the students, we have taken care to see that full justice is done to the syllabus as revised by the University. In the course of writing this book we have utilised many sources, books and of course the Internet. We would like to acknowledge and thank all our sources.

We would like to express our gratitude to Shri. Dinesh Bhai Furia and Shri. Jignesh Furia, our publishers who gave us this opportunity to write on such an interesting topic. We too have learnt from the arduous task of writing on a subject that covers a substantial field.

Last but not the least we take this opportunity to thank all the staff of Nirali Prakashan, which includes Nirja Sharma, Prasad Chintakindi, Ilyas Shaikh, Sarika and Ravindra Walodare for their help and assistance in the preparation of the book. Without their help and wholehearted support this book would not have been published.

In spite of sincere efforts, some errors might have crept in the book at some places. We hope that we shall be excused for the same. Any suggestions or comments to improve the text of the book will be highly appreciated.

Authors

Syllabus ...

1. Human Resource Management (6)

Introduction, development of HRM concept, HRD and HRM, Role of HR Manager, structure of HRM dept. Duties and Responsibilities of HR Manager.

2. Trends in HRM (6)

Change in labour force, composition, knowledge, workers, employee empowerment. HRM challenges, strategic issues mergers and acquisitions, TQM, Downsizing, Reengineering, outsourcing, expanding into global marketing, Global workforce.

3. Manpower Planning (8)

Objectives, Need, Importance, Short and Long term, Manpower Planning, Career and succession planning, Sources of recruitment, procedure, basis of selection, interviews, tests, induction, (Discussion of cases in Recruitment and Selection is advised for better understanding of the topic)

4. Savings (12)

Training Need, system approach to training, Education, Training and Development, Training calendar, Return on Training and Investments.

Methods and types of training management, methods of Performance Appraisal, Errors of Appraisal. Merit Rating: Need, Importance and Methods, Promotion, Transfer, Job Description, Job Evaluation, Job Enlargement, Job Enrichment, Job rotation.

5. Recent Trends and Problems in Motivation, Retention, Attrition, Downsizing and Outsourced Manpower (10)

International Human Resource Management.
- Comparison with domestic HRM
- Managing International HRM-activities.
- Multi-culturism.
- Cross Cultural Training (CCT)
- New Terms. HCN, PCN, TCN, Ethnocentric Approach, Polycentric Approach, Geocentric Approach.
- Discussion of Case Studies Advised for Better Understanding of the Subject

Contents ...

1. Human Resource Management	1.1 – 1.28
2. Trends in HRM	2.1 – 2.30
3. Manpower Planning	3.1 – 3.40
4. Training and Development	4.1 – 4.44
5. Recent Trends and Problems in Motivation, Retention, Attrition, Downsizing and Outsourced Manpower	5.1 – 5.34
• University Question Papers	P.1 – P.2

Chapter 1...

Introduction: Human Resource Management

Contents ...

Introduction
- 1.1 Definitions of Human Resource Management
- 1.2 Development of HRM Concept
- 1.3 HRD and HRM
- 1.4 Role of HR Manager
- 1.5 Structure of Human Resource Department
- 1.6 Duties and Responsibilities of the HR Manager
- Points to Remember
- Case Study
- Questions for Discussion
- Questions from Previous Pune University Examinations

Learning Objectives ...

➢ To gain knowledge of the concept of Human Resource Management
➢ To discuss the development of HRM concept
➢ To understand Human Resource Development and its importance in HRM
➢ To learn about the role, duties and responsibilities of a HR Manager
➢ To be aware of the structure of the HRM department

Introduction

Human beings are social animals hence they can by no means survive and work in isolation. It is necessary to plan, develop and manage relations. Since infancy, each and every human being gains knowledge and experience on understanding others and how to behave in every situation in life. Later, this experience and knowledge is used for managing relations at the workplace.

The whole concept of Human Resource Management revolves around the theme of managing relations at the workplace. Since mid 1980's Human Resource Management (HRM) has gained recognition academically and commercially.

In the current scenario, with the liberation of the Indian economy and its general and halting integration with the world economy the human resource concept suddenly has gained momentum. India has specially carved a place for itself due to the abundant manpower available at low cost.

Today the HR department plays a vital role. There is now an emphasis on trying to build strong and stable HR systems and processes which will provide security to the people. In the current environment, competitive pressures are forcing companies to render cost effective products and services with care and concern for the customer needs. The need is to have competent staff that are flexible enough to respond to the changing demands of the organisation and are integrated and concerned with the mission and survival of the organisation.

The main objective of HRM is to make optimum use of employees' contribution in order to achieve maximum efficiency and output, while at the same time achieving individualistic objectives such as having a challenging job and getting recognition and societal objectives like paying taxes and demonstrating social responsibility.

1.1 Definitions of Human Resource Management

(1) **Prof. Cynthia D. Fisher, Lyle F. Schoenfeldt and James B. Shaw** state that, *"HRM involves all management decisions and practices that directly affect or influence the people or human resources who work for the organisation. In recent years, increasing attention has been devoted to how the organisations manage human resources. It is important to examine as to how organisation's employees enable an organisation to achieve its goals".*

(2) **According to Prof. Wendell L. French, University of Washington**, *"HRM is the term increasingly used for the philosophy, policies, procedures and practices related to the management of people working in an organisation".*

(3) **Prof. K. Aswathappa** makes it clear that, *"Human Resources Management is a management function that helps managers' recruit, select, train and develop members for an organisation. Obviously, HRM is concerned with people's dimension in organisation".*

(4) **According to Prof. George T. Milkovich and Prof. John W. Boudreau**, *"Human Resource Management is a series of decisions that affect the relationship between employees and employers; it affects many aspects and is intended to influence the effectiveness and abilities of employees and employers to achieve their objectives.*

(5) **Prof. C. B. Mamoria and Prof. S. V. Gankar** have stated a very simple and easily understandable definition of HRM which is, *"Human Resource Management is concerned with the people who work in the organisation to achieve the objectives of the organisation. It concerns with the acquisition of appropriate human resources, developing their skills and competencies, motivating them for best performance and ensuring their continued commitment to the organisation to achieve its objectives".* According to them, this definition applies to all types of organisations - industry, business, government, education, health or social welfare of the people.

(6) **According to Prof. Gary Dessler of the Florida International University**, all managers have to perform certain basic functions viz., planning, organising, staffing, leading, controlling etc. These functions, in fact, represent the management process. In his opinion, *"Human Resource Management is the process of acquiring, training, appraising and compensating employees and attending to their labour relations, health and safety and fairness concerns".*

(7) **Ivancevich and Glueek** stated that, *"Human Resource Management is the function performed in organisations that facilitates the most effective use of people (employees) to achieve organisational and individual goals".*

(8) **According to Dale Yoder**, *"The management of human resources is viewed as a system in which participants seek to attain both individual and group goals".*

(9) **According to David Decenzo and Stephen Robbins**, *"Human Resource Management is concerned with the people dimension in management. Since every organisation is made up of people, acquiring their services, developing their skills, motivating them to high level of performance and ensuring that they continue to maintain their commitment to the organisation are essential to achieve organisational objectives. This is true, regardless of the type of organisation, government, business, education, health, recreation or social action".*

(10) **According to Michael VP**, *"Human Resource Management is that part of management process which develops and manages the human elements of enterprise considering the resourcefulness of the people employed in organisation in terms of total knowledge, skills, creative abilities, talents, aptitudes and potentialities for actuating effectively".*

Objectives of HRM

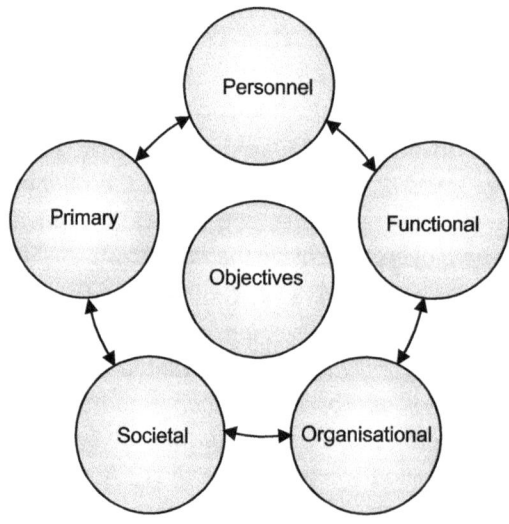

Fig. 1.1

The primary objective of HRM is to ensure the availability of a competent and willing and able work force. HRM objectives can be defined as fivefold:

1. Primary
2. Personnel
3. Functional
4. Organisational objectives
5. Societal objectives.

(1) Primary objectives of HRM are to select the right person at the right time in the right position and in the right place.

(2) Personal objectives of employees must be met if employees are to be maintained, retained and motivated.

(3) Functional objectives remind the HRM that it has functional value which should be fulfilled in an efficient manner.

(4) Organisational objectives are the means to assist the organisation with the primary objectives and to fulfil it in a proper way.

(5) Societal Objectives: Every organisation need to have a responsibility towards the society. The requirements of the society should be maintained and considered. The legal matters should be in accordance with the rules and regulations of the society.

The above mentioned basic objectives generate several other objectives of HRM such as meeting the needs, values, dignity etc. of the employees, proper staffing at all levels of the organisation, training and developing available human resources at all levels, creating high-performing work culture, improving quality of work life, and so on. Thus, the objectives of HRM are derived from the basic objectives of an organisation which are mentioned below:

(1) To create an able and motivated workforce and ensure its effective utilisation to accomplish various organisational goals.

(2) To establish and maintain suitable and sound organisational structure in order to secure integration of employees and groups and to create desirable working relationship amongst them for increasing the organisational effectiveness. For this purpose, efforts are required to be made to create a sense and feeling of belongingness and team spirit by encouraging the employees to make positive and valuable suggestions.

(3) To create an environment that would help maintain high morale and to encourage a value system that would foster trust and mutuality of interests.

(4) To provide training and education for developing human resources.

(5) To provide opportunities for participation, recognition, etc., and for a fair, acceptable and efficient leadership.

(6) To provide attractive incentives, monetary benefits, social security measures and welfare facilities, various non-monetary rewards, benefits, etc., in order to ensure the retention of competent employees.

(7) To adopt such policies which recognise merits and contributions by the employees.

(8) To ensure that there is no threat of unemployment by instilling confidence among the employees regarding stability of their employment.

(9) An organisation has to bear in mind its responsibility towards the society as a whole. The society may not desire to enforce reservation in hiring and the laws leading to discrimination affecting the society badly or if certain organisational decisions have some negative impact on the society, such decisions should be avoided. It should be the objective of an organisation to use the resources for the betterment of the society and the nation.

(10) To develop and maintain a quality work life which makes employment in the organisation a desirable, personal and social situation.

1.2 Development of HRM Concept

Evolution of the HRM Concept

YEAR 1800

The concept of Human Resource came into existence after 1800. Human resource management was concerned with the terms of employment, health schemes, and home for the lady employee's children.

YEAR 1950

Following the Second World War, Human Resource Management had a wider scope for variety of services, including wages management, training and guidance on industrial relations. The increasing organisational size was responsible for certain change in industrial relation practices.

YEAR 1960-1970

The 1960s and 1970s saw a notable increase in the number of staff engaged in human resource work. This could be attributable in part to an increase in the amount of employment legislation. However, the state of the economy had a part to play as well. In conditions of full employment, up to the early 1970s, there was indication of much staffing, selection, training and payment system activities in the practice of human resource management. This was encouraged to some extent by labour shortages, and was reflected in actions to be dependent on skilled labour and increase the skill levels of the work-force.

The concept of training was well-organised and considered, heavily subjective by the enterprise of the training boards, which exacted a training level from industry and offered grants to companies that conducted training to acceptable standards. That led to a rapid growth in the number of training specialists within the personnel function. Welfare personnel was concerned with the provision of schemes, considered progressive at that time, dealing with unemployment, sick pay and subsidised housing for employees.

The beginning of these schemes could be viewed as a response to the severity of capitalism at that period of British history. Indeed, today it could be distinguished that the welfare custom has some importance in the act of staff administration, for instance, health plans and day nurture the kids of women employees. Personnel administration ended up as backing for administration and was essentially concerned with recruitment, restrain, punctuality, frameworks, preparing and keeping work records for prospective exercises, for example performance appraisal and planning future manpower needs had picked up significance so that the future development could be administered. The attention on industrial relations proclaimed a fragile part for the staff communicating with both the administration and labourers.

YEAR 1980

The 1980s human resource or personnel management entered the industrial stage of adjusting itself to the business sector economy and capitalistic society. It was not exceptional to find senior personnel executives helping the organisation about its future identified with the importance of existing business goals, and enhanced methods for attaining revised goals. Shortcoming in the force of trade unions indicated the need for less expands forms in collective bargaining and conflict management. It likewise leads to swifter arranged pay settlements. Also, organisations were better placed to make changes in work practices which resulted in increased productivity and a reduction in the numbers employed. There were changes in personnel practices due to the large pool of available labour. For example, the importance switched from recruitment attracting candidates to selection. It was during the 1980s that the rise in HRM began to attract the attention of personnel practitioners. There was a move away from the traditionally adversarial industrial relations of the 1970s towards an approach which sought to achieve excellence in the organisation through a committed work-force.

YEAR 1990

The early 1990s witnessed a change in emphasis. The reaction to individualism and unforgivable greed of the 1980s had made way for the spirit of consent and the value of teamwork. There was a fear in the mind of the core workers because high commitment is required from these workers. They are expected to be flexible about the hours they work and to work above and beyond their job descriptions. Wages tend to reflect the market rate rather than the rate determined by agreements with trade unions.

Today's HR profession encompasses a number of specialised disciplines, including variety, reward (including compensation, benefits, pensions), resourcing, employee relations, organisation development and design, and learning and development.

Human Resources Management in Modern Times (Global Perspective)

The roots of HRM in modern times go back to the pioneering work of **Drucker** (1955) and **McGregor** in the 1960s. **Drucker** (1955) virtually invented management by objectives (although he never actually used that phrase). He wrote that, *'An effective management must direct the vision and efforts of all managers towards a common goal.'* This concept of visionary, goal-directed leadership is fundamental to HRM. He castigated personnel managers for their obsession with techniques that become gimmicks and for their inability to get really involved in business. And he referred to personnel management as *'a collection of individual techniques without much internal cohesion – a hodge podge.'*

The emphasis in the HRM approach on coherence and internal consistency follows the Drucker line. He also stressed that human resource should be regarded as an organisational asset, thus expressing what later become the basic philosophy of HRM.

McGregor (1960) advocated management by integration and self control as a strategy for managing people which affects the whole business. A key role of the personal function, as he saw it, was to 'devise means of getting management to examine its assumptions, to consider the consequences and to compare it with others.'

Like Drucker, McGregor, therefore, paved the way for the evolution of the basic HRM concept that human resource plans must be integrated with those of the business. The behavioural science movement came into prominence in the 1960s. Its leading architects were as follows:

(a) **Maslow** (1954), whose hierarchy of human needs places self-actualisation at the top of the pyramid.

(b) **Likert** (1966), who developed the integration principle of supporting relationships. This states that organisation member should, in the light of their values and expectations, view their work as supportive and as contributing to the building and maintenance of their sense of personal worth and importance.

(c) **Argyris** (1957), who believed that organisational design should plan for integration and movement and that individuals should feel that they have a high degree of self-control over setting their own goals and over the paths defining those goals.

(d) **Herzberg** (1957) who advocated job enrichment as a means of improving organisational effectiveness.

Although, the behavioural science movement had a somewhat idealistic flavour about it, it did make two useful contributions to HRM. First, it underlined the importance of integration and involvement and secondly, it highlighted the idea that management should as a basic value accept the need to improve the quality of working life as a means of obtaining better motivation and improved results.

Development of the Concept of Human Resource in India

HRM in India is centuries old. The first reference of HRM was provided by Kautilya as early as 4th century B.C. in his book *'Arthashastra'*. The work environment had logical procedures and principles in respect of labour organisation such as *'Shreni'* Wages were paid in terms of quantity and quality of work. Workers were punished for unnecessary delay or spoiling of work. Kautilya's contribution was based on *Shamrastra* Concepts like job description, qualifications for jobs, selection procedures, executive development, incentive system and performance appraisal were very effectively analysed and explained.

The guild system prevailed in the Indian economy too. It was based on *Varnashram* or caste system and resulted in division of labour accordingly. In the course of time, professions became hereditary. From 14th century B.C. to the latter half of 10th century B.C., the relationship of employer-employee was marked with justice and equity.

During the Mughal rule, *Karkhanas'* were established, but the artisans and craftsmen were poor and lived on starvation level and the productivity was low.

During the British rule, the work environment was appalling and full of inhuman cruelties. This continued till 1881 when the Factory Act was enacted. This Act provided for (i) weekly holidays (ii) fixation of working hours (iii) fixation of minimum age for children at 7 years subject to a maximum working period of 7 hours a day.

A further powerful effect on the managerial history of India was to be provided by the British system of corporate organisation for 200 years. Clearly, the socio cultural roots of Indian heritage are diverse and have been drawn from multiple sources including ideas brought from other parts of the old world. Interestingly, these ideas were essentially secular even when they originated from religious bases.

Till 1960, recruitment was untouched by law but the rapid growth of industry and the consequent demand for skilled and semi-skilled workers led to the government enacting the Employment Exchange Act, 1959, to regulate recruitment of workers and the Apprentice Act, 1961, to regulate the training of workers to some extent.

Thus, human resource management in India began with industrial discipline and getting rid of troublemakers. At a later stage, personnel officers were appointed as "labour welfare officers" to satisfy statutory requirements.

Later, the role of a personnel officer was converted into that of an "industrial relations officer". Today, his role is that of a "human resource manager". He works in the three areas- labour welfare, industrial relations and personnel administration.

1.3 HRD AND HRM

HRM stands for human resources management, which means the art of managing all aspects of the human work force at a company or organisation.

HRM aims at providing a best working environment for employees to fully utilise their talent to their best to achieve the company's future output. As human resources usually apply to big companies and organisations, it has sub categories, among which is HRD, which stands for human resources development.

HRD is a component of HRM that focuses on nurturing employee's skills. The process of hiring new employees can be long and expensive hence most companies employ the strategy of HRD to promote endurance of employees within the company because through this an employee is likely to progressively scale up the managerial ladder.

Human resources management of a company is often a self-regulating department of its own composed of various sections including recruitment and retention, performance and appraisal management, HRD and compensation sections. But HRD does not only focus on development of skills but also focuses on the personal development of staff. Because employees needs and expectations are ever growing and changing this section of HRM is specifically there to help employees cope with such and prepare them for future reservations.

Generally speaking, professionals working within the HRM department must have excellent skills although this is more so with those particularly working in the HRD section. The HRD section needs to have professionals with flawless people management skills as they need to be able to understand talent within people from a cross section of backgrounds. The HRD section is concerned with identifying strengths and weaknesses among different employees and providing training which will make those skills complement the other.

Human Resource Development (HRD)

Human Resource Development (HRD) is the framework to help employees develop their personal and organisational skills, knowledge, and abilities.

Human Resource Development includes opportunities as employee training, employee career development, performance management and development, coaching, mentoring, succession planning, key employee identification, tuition assistance, and organisation development.

The focus of all aspects of Human Resource Development is on developing the most superior workforce so that the organisation and individual employees can accomplish their work goals in service to customers.

HRD programmes create a team of well-trained, efficient and capable managers and subordinates. Such team constitutes an important asset of an enterprise. One organisation is different from another mainly because of the people (employees) working therein.

According to **Peter F. Drucker**, "*the prosperity, if not the survival of any business depends on the performance of its managers of tomorrow.*" The human resource should be nurtured and used for the benefit of the organisation. Organisations have many opportunities for human resources or employee development, both within and outside of the workplace.

Human Resource Development can be formal such as in classroom training, a college course, or an organisational planned change effort. Or, Human Resource Development can be informal as in employee coaching by a manager. Healthy organisations believe in Human Resource Development and cover all of these bases.

Human resource development in the organisation is therefore a process by which the employees of an organisation are helped, in a continuous and planned way. HRD is a process, not merely a set of rules and regulations. There are many activities such as performance appraisal, counselling, training and organisation development interventions are used to initiate, facilitate and promote the process is a continuous way.

Human Resource Development (HRD) has gained increasing attention in the last few decades from human resource specialists, training and development professionals, chief executives.

Many dimensions of HRD has been integrated into research, training and organisational design if the management people or consultants are to utilise this knowledge effectively.

HRD is required by all organisations that want to be dynamic and growth oriented. Organisations can become dynamic only through the efforts and competencies of their human resources. Employee capabilities must be continuously acquired, sharpened and explored. When the employees use their talent, initiative, take risk, experiment, innovate and make things happen, the organisation, may be said to have an enabling culture. HRD is a function more concerned with training and development, career planning and development and organisation development. HRD is thus a part of HRM.

Elements of Human Resource Development and their Inter-relationship/Systems of HRD

(a) Career Planning and Development: Career Planning is one of the most important functions of the personnel department. It means the programmes and the procedures which are designed to provide the individual leverage in deciding their personal career within the environment of the organisation. Career planning helps to facilitate dialogue between the individual and the organisation for optimising their mutual requirements. Career planning, stands for the forward looking employment policies of an organisation which take into account the career of individual executives involved in various tasks, particularly the critical tasks. It unites organisational human resource planning with individual career needs. The career planning programme should be dynamic. Promotion means the assignment of a position of higher responsibility to an individual. Transfer is the change in jobs which may involve some changes in status, responsibilities and salary, etc.

(b) Performance Appraisal: Performance appraisal is one of the oldest and most universal practices of management. It refers to all the formal procedures used in working organisations to evaluate the personalities, contributions and potential of the group members. It is to improve but not to prove work performance. It can serve as a basis for change or promotion. It serves as a feedback to the employee. Performance appraisal often provides the rational foundation for the payment of piece-work, wages, bonus etc. It is also used as a guide for formulating an appropriate training and development programme to improve the quality of performance of an employee in his present work. Performance appraisal often serves as a means for evaluating the effectiveness of devices for the selection and classification of workers.

(c) Potential Appraisal: Potential appraisal as a sub-system of HRD is created to judge the potential abilities of the employees as well as the executives. Under it, the capacity of the person in respect of technical skills and knowledge, aptitude for a particular type of work, willingness to take initiative, motivation, level of intelligence and willingness to accept responsibility is ascertained. By using this information, management can identify persons having potentiality for doing more responsible jobs. Such persons already possess a certain capacity and by giving them further training such capacity can be developed to the required level so that when the need arises they can be promoted to the higher posts in the organisation. Potential appraisal also helps the employees because they become aware of the skills, abilities and aptitudes they have and can make efforts for developing and using them in the future.

(d) Training: An organisation which undertakes human resource development has to establish a system for the training of its employees. Training is an instrument of developing the employees by increasing their skills and by improving their behaviour. Technical, managerial skills are needed by the employees for performing the jobs assigned to them. Training is required to be given to new employees as well as the experienced employees. The methods to be used for training and the duration for which training should be given is decided by the management in keeping with the objectives of the training, the number of persons to be trained and the amount of training needed by the employees.

Training is concerned with skill formation and improvement in a narrow sense, but in a broader sense, it refers to all the procedures that lead to the overall personal development. The major outcome of training is learning. Trainees learn new habits, new skills and useful knowledge that helps them improve their performance.

(e) Organisational Development: Organisational Development is the process of employing various methods and techniques by which an organisation develops and is able to survive and make progress in the changing environment. The people working in the organisation should by developed by increasing their skills, abilities and capacity to adjust themselves to the changed environment. In organisation development, efforts are made for team-building and creativity of organisational culture so that the performance of the people can be improved. For organisational development, the organisation should be willing to change itself according to the need created by the changes in the environment in which it operates.

Organisational Development (OD) has emerged to help the planned change for organisational effectiveness. Thus, it is said that organisational development is the modern approach to management of change and human resource development. Organisational Development (OD) concentrates on people dimensions like norms, values, attitudes, relationships, organisational climate etc. Different managers view differently and various authors have given a variety of definitions about OD.

Goals or Objectives of Human Resource Development

(A) Goals in Respect of the Organisation

(i) **Development of Employees and preparing them for Acceptance of Additional Responsibilities:** HRD activity is undertaken by the management of an organisation mainly for developing its existing employees. The employees may have some deficiencies in terms of skill or ability required to perform the jobs satisfactorily. By identifying such deficiencies, the management selects the appropriate training and development programmes for the particular employees. This helps the organisation in obtaining employees capable of performing their jobs. Once the required level of competence and skill has been acquired by the employee, he is given more responsible work. Thus, to satisfy manpower needs of the organisation at higher levels, HRD activity may be started by the organisation.

(ii) **Welcome the Change and Adapt to it:** Every organisation has to function in an environment in which changes of different nature and in different fields continuously take place. The success of the organisation depends upon its ability to face these changes and adapt itself as per the change in the situation. HRD activity may be undertaken by the management with the objective of modifying the structure of the organisation. Organisation is made up of the people working in it. Therefore, the objective behind HRD would be to develop employees who can accept the changes in the environment and adjust their working accordingly.

(iii) **Implementation of the Programme of 'Total Quality Management':** An organisation's objective in undertaking HRD activity is to improve the working of it in every field. Improvement in the working is possible only when the employees working in different departments become area of the need for improvement and their capacity is improved for doing the work. HRD results in increasing the capacity of the employees so that they can carry out innovative work, find out better methods and techniques for production and marketing of the output and thus achieve the objective of the total quality management.

(iv) Maintenance of Sound Human Relations: HRD creates the awareness among the management that humanisation of the organisation is essential. Executives gain information about their employees and become aware of their needs. They start treating the employees as human being who has feelings and emotions. They start to undertake programmes for developing the employees and once the employees realise that their superiors care for them and treat them with dignity and respect, they also begin to reciprocate and in this manner, sound human relations are developed in the organisation.

(B) Goals in Respect of the Individuals

(i) **Development of Potential:** All the employees possess certain skills, abilities and capacities. Depending upon the need of the work, they use these to some extent but may not use them in the full extent. In HRD activity, efforts are made to ascertain about the potentials of the individual employees and therefore unused or dormant qualities of the employees are brought to the surface. Then efforts are made to make use of them for the benefit of the individual employee as well as the organisation.

(ii) **Increase in Performance:** In HRD activity, efforts are made on a continuous basis to achieve improvement in the performance of the employees. Through performance appraisal the performance of the employee is judged and any beneficence in the performance is ascertained. Then systematic efforts are made to remove the reasons due to which the performance of the employee has remained below the expected standard. Educating and training the employee helps him to do his job in a better way and increase in his performance is achieved.

(iii) **Fulfillment of Needs:** An individual employee has various needs. When HRD programmes are undertaken by the management it pays greater attention to each individual employee. His behaviour is studied and information about his needs and expectations is obtained. HRD succeeds only when the individual employees becomes satisfied and contented. To achieve this objective, the management makes efforts to provide better working conditions, adequate remuneration and opportunities to participate in management. Formation of formal and informal groups of the employees is encouraged and job satisfaction is provided to the employees. All these efforts are made to fulfil the various needs of the employees.

(C) Goals in Respect of Groups

(i) **Increase in Cooperation:** In any organisation, the employees are divided into groups for performing different activities related to the work. When employees work in the group they need to work together and co-operate with each other. It is the goal of HRD to increase the co-operation amongst the members of the group as well as between different groups. HRD helps the employees understand each other better. When HRD increases the abilities of the employees, the confidence of the employees in each other increases and better cooperation in the members of the groups becomes possible. HRD helps to develop team-spirit which also increases cooperation from the employees.

(ii) Creation of Collaboration and Team Effectiveness: HRD activity is undertaken by the management to obtain collaboration from the groups of employees and for increasing their team-effectiveness. An organisational culture is developed due to HRD which creates such collaboration. Groups of employees develop good relations with the management and help the management in achieving objectives of the organisation in a more effective way.

1.4 Role of HR Manager

The HR manager creates an infrastructure in the organisation that affects employees, customers, supplier and investors. The HR practices must be in alignment with the organisation's goals. The HR manager values people and works to create both a competitive and compassionate group. They should develop competencies and play appropriate roles. HR people always need to think ahead of times and think something positive and beneficial for the organisation. The HR manager is usually top ranking personnel who administers and coordinates across functional areas.

Human resources managers handle personnel decisions, including hiring, position assignment, training, benefits, and compensation. Their decisions are subject to some oversight, but company executives recognise their experience and skill in assessing personnel and rely heavily on their recommendations.

Although physical resources-capital, building, equipment are important, most companies realise that the quality and quantity of their output is directly related to the quality and commitment of their personnel.

Human resources professionals make sure that appropriate matches are made between support staff and producers, between assistants and managers, and between co-workers to enhance productivity, support the company's business strategy and long-term goals, and provide a satisfying work experience for employees.

A human resources professional in a smaller firm is involved in hiring, resource allocation, compensation, benefits, and compliance with laws and regulations affecting employees and the workplace and safety and health issues. This multiplicity of tasks requires individuals with strong organisational skills who can quickly shift from project to project and topic to topic without becoming overwhelmed.

Strong interpersonal skills are crucial for managers at small firms. These managers spend much of their day handling questions, attending budgeting and strategic planning meetings, and interviewing prospective employees. The rest of the time, they take care of paperwork and talk on the telephone with service providers (insurance, health care, bank officers, etc.).

At larger firms, human resources managers often specialise in one area, such as compensation, hiring, or resources allocation. Compensation analysts work with department managers to determine pay scales and bonus structures. Hiring specialists (also known as recruiters) place ads in appropriate publications, review resumes, and interview candidates for employment. Allocation managers match assistants, support staff, and other employees with departments that have specific needs. Sensitivity to both personality issues and corporate efficiency are a plus for allocation managers.

The most difficult feature of the human resources professional's job is handling the dirty work involved in the staffing of a company: dealing with understaffing, refereeing disputes between two mismatched personalities, firing employees, informing employees of small (or nonexistent) bonuses, maintaining an ethical culture, and reprimanding irresponsible employees. Performing these tasks can be disheartening for human resources managers who are supposed to support and assist employees, and many human resources managers feel that employees dislike or fear them because of this role.

Various functions which are performed by a human resource manager have the basic objective to bring together expertise in the most scientific way and also to create the attitudes that motivate the people in the organisation to achieve the goals of the organisation economically, effectively, efficiently and speedily.

From this point of view, human resource managers have to take various decisions regarding the human resources which affect the relationships between employers and employees and also to consider the inter-relationships among these decisions.

It is the primary function of a human resource manager to manage the human resources of his organisation to attain the objectives of the organisation. From the primary responsibilities of human resource manager enumerated below, we get an idea about the functions or duties he has to perform.

(a) To create and utilise an able and motivated work force to accomplish the basic organisational goals.

(b) To establish and maintain sound organisational structure and desirable working relationships among all the members of the organisation.

(c) To secure the integration of individuals and groups within the organisation by coordination of the individual and group goals with those of the organisation.

(d) To create facilities and opportunities for individual and group development so as to match it with the growth of the organisation.

(e) To affect an effective utilisation of the human resource for the achievement of organisational goals.

(f) To identify and satisfy individual and group needs by providing adequate and equitable wages, incentives, employee benefits and social security and measures to provide challenging work, prestige, recognition, security and status etc.

(g) To maintain high employee morale and sound human relations by sustaining and improving the various conditions and facilities.

(h) To strengthen and appreciate the human assets continuously by providing training and developmental programmes.

(i) To consider and contribute to the minimisation of socio-economic evils such as unemployment, under-employment, inequalities in the distribution of income and wealth and to improve the welfare of the society by providing employment opportunities to women and disadvantaged sections of the society etc.

(j) To provide an opportunity to the employees for their expression and voice in management.

(k) To provide fair, acceptable and efficient leadership.

(l) To provide facilities and conditions of work and creation of favourable atmosphere for maintaining stability of employment.

(m) To design and develop structured learning programmes to help to accelerate learning for employees and their groups.

(n) HR Manager has to take many decisions which affect the relationships between the employers and employees. For example, how many employees to be appointed at what levels of skills and experience (Recruitment), whom to be trained and promoted (promotion), how much to pay, how to tackle the general problems of the employees and to handle dissatisfied employees etc. Many decisions are very complex and complicated. HR Manager's role is very important in this respect and he has to take decisions very carefully.

(o) To design suitable HR Systems for producing maximum impact on organisational performance and development.

(p) To identify and develop suitable HRD strategies in harmony with overall business strategy.

(q) To provide support services for the implementation of HRD programmes effectively.

(r) To take necessary steps to ensure the full and optimum use of available resources and competencies and to create commitment among the people working in and for the organisation to meet consumer's needs. There must be smoothest flow of products and services to consumers; otherwise the consumers cannot be satisfied.

(s) To evaluate the impact of HRD practices and programmes practiced and to communicate their results for further development.

(t) To suggest long-term strategies for organisational excellence.

1.5 Structure of Human Resource Department

Increasing importance of human resources is realised by the management of business and industrial concerns and therefore, for the management of human resources, a separate department known as 'Human Resource Department' is created in the organisational structure of these concerns or enterprises.

The organisation or structure of the Human Resource Department depends upon the size of the enterprise, form of the organisation adopted and the types of the activities to be carried out by the department. The management of the enterprise decides how the HR Department should be organised and in how many sections, it should be divided. As per the needs, additional sections are created or some sections are combined for the purposes of carrying out the functions of the department.

Organisational Structure of the HRM Department

The internal organisational structure of the HRM department varies widely in different companies, depending upon their size. In small companies the function of the HRM department are limited and restricted. Their may be two or three people working in the department. In case of a large organisation the functions carried out by the HRM department are many and varied. A number of people work in various levels and carry out the working of the entire company. HRM unit or department works on three categories:

1. Functional basis
2. Service basis
3. Client basis.

Structure of HRM Department

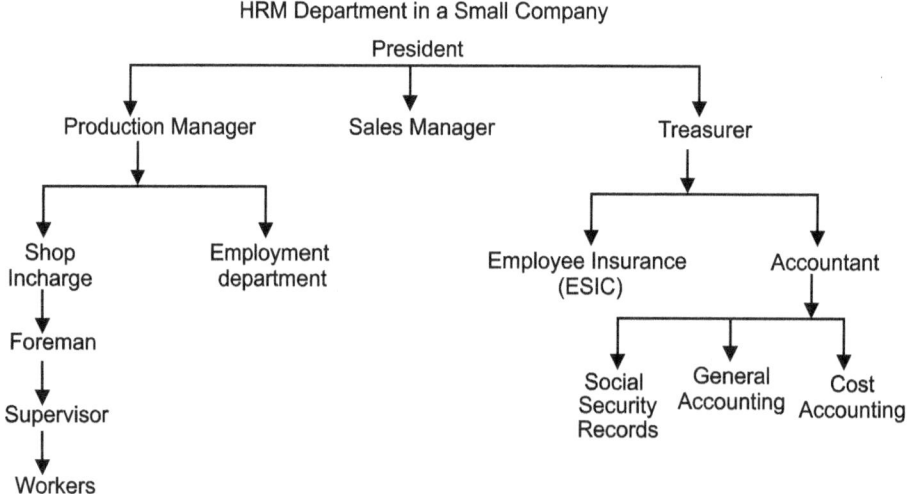

Fig 1.2

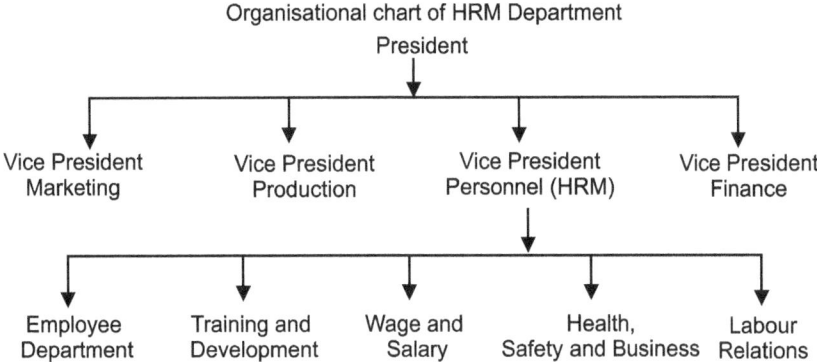

Fig 1.3

1. Functional basis: Departments are grouped into different functions such as employment, training, wage of salary administration, labour relations, safety and employee services and retirement. All the work would be influenced on the size of the organisation, top management philosophy etc.

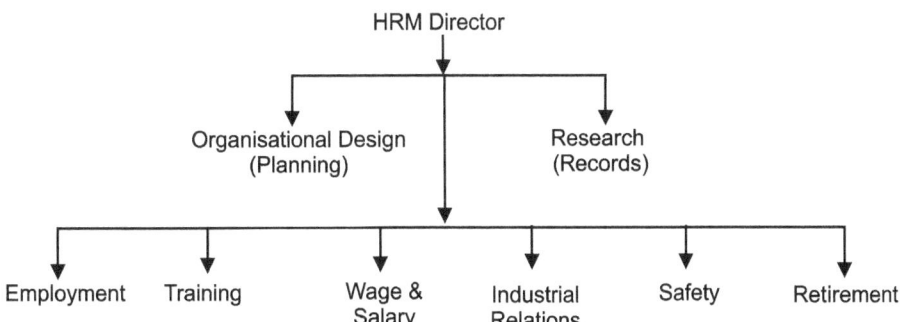

Fig 1.4

2. Service basis: This basis takes into consideration the service rendered. It tries to improve the satisfaction of the employee's through various ways like hygienic maintenance, motivational programmes etc. It is very essential to take the employees into confidence and get the work done from them. This comes from the feeling of belongingness which is very essential. If the employees understand that the organisation is working for them and their interest and developments are taken care of. The satisfaction level of the employees increases. This is very beneficial to the organisation.

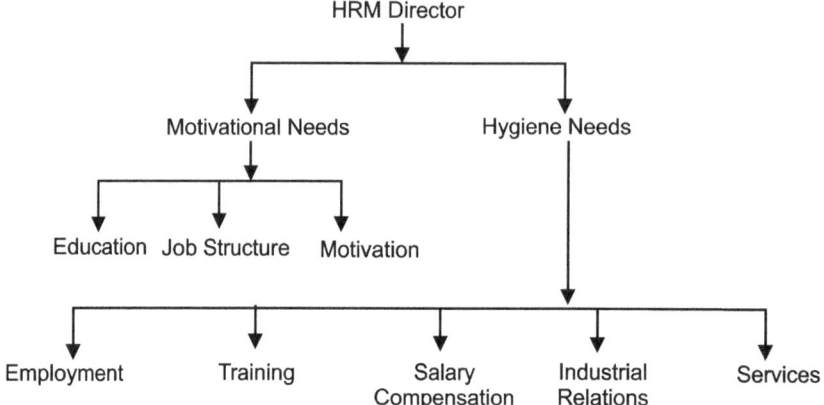

Fig 1.5

3. **Clientele basis:**

Fig. 1.6

Organisation Structure

Organisations are collection of and inter-related among people, machines, materials systems, information and other resources. The inter-linkage among these resources results in synergy. Division of labour enables the employees to specialise in a particular job. Organisations structured around narrow-width jobs results in vertical structures and structured around wider. Width jobs result in flat structures.

Vertical/Tall Organisations, refer to increase in the length of the organisation's hierarchical chain of command. The hierarchical chain of command represents the company's authority accountability relationship between superiors and subordinates. Authority and responsibility flow from the top to the bottom through all the levels of the hierarchy. Accountability flows from the lowest level to the highest level. Employees at each level should report to their superiors. Authority is centralised in tall organisations.

Horizontal/Flat Organisations, refer to an increase in breadth of an organisation's structure the number of levels in the organisation are few. The span of control is relatively large.

Steps in Designing Organisational Structure

The first step in organisation design is analysis of present and future circumstances and environmental factors. Company analysis is the basis for organisation design and is the process of defining aims, objectives, activities and structure of an enterprise. Organisational analysis includes an analysis of the following aspects:

1. **External Environment:** Social, technical, economic, political and natural factors.
2. **Overall Aims and Objectives of the Enterprise:** Survival, growth, profit maximisation, wealth maximisation etc.
3. **Objectives:** Specific goals to be achieved.
4. **Activities:** What needs to be performed.
5. **Decisions:** To be taken across vertical and horizontal dimensions.
6. **Relationships:** From the team point and communication point.
7. **Job structure:** Job design, job description, job specification.
8. **Organisational climate:** Working atmosphere of the company.
9. **Human resource:** Availability of human resources marked by skill, knowledge, commitment etc.

Approaches to Organisational Structure

There are nine approaches to structure the organisation. They are:

1. Entrepreneurial structure
2. Functional organisational structure
3. Product organisational structure
4. Geographical organisational structure
5. Customer based organisational structure
6. Strategic business unit structure
7. Line and staff structure divisions
8. Matrix organisational structure
9. Team structure.

(1) **Entrepreneurial Structure:** These types of organisations don't require an organisational chart and formal assignment of responsibilities. The owner-manager who is performing all functions in the initial stage has to perform more managerial activities than operational activities.

(2) **Functional Organisational Structure:** Each functional department consists of those jobs in which employees perform similar jobs at different levels. The different functions are marketing, finance, HR, manufacturing, R & D, engineering etc.

(3) **Product Organisational Structure:** Companies producing more than one product structure their organisations based on product structures. Normally activities are divided on the basis of individual products, product line, services and are grouped into departments. All the important functions are performed within the department only.

(4) **Geographical Organisation Structure:** The functions are grouped into departments based on the activities performed in geographical areas. Each geographical unit includes all functions required to produce and market the products in a particular geographical area. This structure is used by chain stores, power companies', restaurants chain, dairy products, banking etc.

(5) **Customer Based Structure:** Some companies with significant customer base, structure their organisations based on customers. Customers and their use of the product/services are the key aspects in product design, marketing practices and services.

(6) **Strategic Business Unit Structure:** A strategic business unit is a grouping of business subsidiaries based on some important strategic elements common to each. Top management co-ordinates the interests of the diversified business units. The business can be effectively controlled if they are related business grouped into strategic units and the efficient and senior executive is delegated with the authority and responsibility for its management.

(7) **Line and Staff Organisation:** The relationships with which the managers in an organisation deal with one another are broadly classified into two categories line and staff. In a line and staff organisations, the work of administration of business units is divided into two broad divisions - the staff which is responsible for planning and the line for the actual execution of the work. The staff is attached to the line to assist the line in discharging its duties efficiently. The staff officials prepare plans and recommend to the line officials who implement them with the help of their departmental personnel. The line and staff organisation is based on the principle of specialisation.

(8) **Matrix Organisation:** Structure possesses a dual chain of command. Both functional and project managers exercise authority over organisational activities in a matrix structure. Therefore personnel in this structure have two superiors namely the project manager and the manager of the functional department. The matrix structure is commonly used in the firms whose technical change is rapid.

(9) **Team Structure:** It takes three forms:
   (i) Project team
   (ii) Task force team
   (iii) Venture team

Project team is created to handle special kind of situations with a finite life expectancy. Project teams are self-sufficient work groups. These are created to supervise the completion of a special activity. The setting up of a new technology process, starting up a new venture, producing a new product, initiating and completion of a joint venture are examples of project teams.

Task force team consists of top level executives and specialists in different areas from the organisation who caters to specific events only.

Venture team is a group of individuals. The purpose of forming this team is to bring a specific product or a new business entity.

1.6 Duties and Responsibilities of the HR Manager

The Human Resource Manager leads and directs the HR team to enable them to deliver a comprehensive HR service to the business. The HR Manager proactively advises on best HR practice and wherever necessary takes a hands-on role in dealing with case work.

The HR Manager supports the people management functions that underpin the business culture. The broad areas include: employee matters, compensation and benefits, reward, professional growth, communications and performance management.

Duties of HR Manager

Lead and direct the Human Resource team to deliver a comprehensive HR service to the business

- **Employee Relations:** Managing absence, disciplinary, grievances, sickness etc. Measure employee satisfaction and identify areas that require improvement.
- **Performance Management:** Coaching managers on performance management issues and processes.
- **Learning and Development:** Providing guidance on development for managers and their teams.
- **Training:** Implementing the training and development agenda; identify areas that need attention and improvement.
- **Recruitment and retention:** Managing talent and succession planning; taking overall responsibility for recruitment activity and campaigns.
- Reward advice and support employees on company benefits.
- Implementing policy and procedures of new HR policies, procedures and processes.
- In conjunction with the Head of HR, ensure all company policies and procedures are up to date in line with current employment law. Ensure line managers are up to date with changes to any policies.
- Working with senior managers, coaching them and advising on all people issues.

- Deal with complex disciplinary/grievance and HR issues, using HR and company knowledge evidencing appropriate decision making skills.
- Crafting of business and people solutions.
- Managing priorities between casework and projects.
- Managing HR budgets.
- Allocate human resources, ensuring appropriate matches between personnel.
- Provide current and prospective employees with information about policies, job duties, working conditions, wages, opportunities for promotion and employee benefits.
- Perform difficult staffing duties, including dealing with understaffing, refereeing disputes, firing employees, and administering disciplinary procedures.
- Advise managers on organisational policy matters such as equal employment opportunity and sexual harassment, and recommend needed changes.
- Analyse and modify compensation and benefits policies to establish competitive programs and ensure compliance with legal requirements.
- Plan and conduct new employee orientation to foster positive attitude toward organisational objectives.
- Serve as a link between management and employees by handling questions, interpreting and administering contracts and helping resolve work-related problems.
- Plan, direct, supervise, and coordinate work activities of subordinates and staff relating to employment, compensation, labour relations, and employee relations.
- Analyse training needs to design employee development, language training and health and safety programmes.
- Maintain records and compile statistical reports concerning personnel-related data such as hires, transfers, performance appraisals, and absenteeism rates.
- Analyse statistical data and reports to identify and determine causes of personnel problems and develop recommendations for improvement of organisation's personnel policies and practices.
- Plan, organise, direct, control or coordinate the personnel, training, or labour relations activities of an organisation.
- Conduct exit interviews to identify reasons for employee termination.
- Investigate and report on industrial accidents for insurance carriers.
- Represent organisation at personnel-related hearings and investigations.
- Negotiate bargaining agreements and help interpret labour contracts.
- Prepare personnel forecast to project employment needs.

- Prepare and follow budgets for personnel operations.
- Develop, administer and evaluate applicant tests.
- Oversee the evaluation, classification and rating of occupations and job positions.
- Study legislation, arbitration decisions, and collective bargaining contracts to assess industry trends.
- Develop and/or administer special projects in areas such as pay equity, savings bond programmes, day-care, and employee awards.
- Provide terminated employees with outplacement or relocation assistance.
- Contract with vendors to provide employee services, such as food service, transportation, or relocation service.

An organisation is a social institution. Its very existence is dependent upon its harmonious relationships with various segments of the society. The process of evolving mutual relationship between firms and various interest groups begins by acknowledging the existence of the responsibilities of a manager. These responsibilities are towards customers, shareholders, employees, suppliers, distributors of retailers, competitors, unions, government and society.

Responsibilities of HR Manager
- Responsibilities towards employees
- Responsibilities towards shareholders
- Responsibilities towards union
- Responsibilities towards government
- Responsibilities towards society
- Responsibilities towards industry

(1) Responsibilities towards Employees: Employees are the most vital resource for any organisation. It is through their hard work, ingenuity, loyalty and dedication that the organisation becomes successful. In return, we have to ensure that we are giving them a fair and reasonable salary and compliance with the statutory obligation of provident fund, gratuity, insurance, bonus etc. Productivity linked bonus and incentives are a way to ensure that the employees can share in the growth and prosperity of the firm.

Apart from wages, provision of a safe, healthy environment which is conducive to work is essential. There must be proper and adequate facilities such as canteen, bathrooms, first aid room etc. The extent and importance of these facilities will vary from organisation to organisation. Realising the importance of a comfortable working environment, many progressive companies have canteens which provide hot wholesome lunch at subsidised rates. Some companies also provide transportation for employees at their own costs. Some companies offer housing and medical facilities to the employees. Development of such amenities is a reflection of the growing realisation by companies that employees are not simply another source of production, but are human beings with emotions, desires, aspirations and have a life outside the company too. Only a happy satisfied human being can be a productive worker. Many organisations extend the facilities to the employee's families also.

According to J. R. D. Tata "One of the inherent drawbacks of modern industry, with its large and concentrated labour forces, is the difficulty of maintaining personal touch between management and employees. As a result, many petty grievances, negligible individually but substantial in the aggregate, which might have been eliminated by a friendly word or timely action are allowed to build up a sense of discontent and frustration among the workers".

As an HR manager ensure that all dealings with the employees are fair. Whether it is determining the profit linked bonus that is being calculated at the provident fund of a retired employee which has to be paid, ensure that the employees are not cheated harassed or humiliated in any form.

(2) Responsibility towards Shareholders: The prime responsibility of the manager is to ensure the security of the shareholders capital. The manager must ensure that the firm does not become bankrupt or it is faced with a situation where the shareholders capital is endangered.

The manager has to ensure that the shareholders are able to earn profit on their capital. Shareholders invest their hard earned savings in the firm with the hope that they will be able to earn more on it than if they keep the money in a bank. Money invested by shareholders is representative of this faith they have in the competence and ability of the organisation. By virtue of the capital invested in the organisation, the shareholders become owners of the company to the proportion of the amount invested.

(3) Responsibility towards Union: The union represents the collective strength of all the individual workers. In dealing with the union the manager must recognise and acknowledge the bargaining power of the union arising out of its collective strength. The union will always bargain with the organisation for maximum benefit. As a manager try not to block this bargaining power but help in providing the union with the correct facts and figures about costs and profits and thus aim for a realistic workable agreement which suit both the parties. Besides providing the correct information attempt to involve the union in the process of managing the firm. You can do this by inviting representatives of the union to sit on the management board. The basic requirement for encouraging participative management is the manager's positive attitude and creation of an atmosphere which encourages free and frank exchange of views among employees and management. Most problems with union arise because of the assumption of the managers that unions have no constructive contribution to make but are interested only in playing a negative role. Appreciate the fact that the management and union have a great degree of mutual dependence and the union cannot further its interests at the cost of the firms interests of vice-versa. Only a relationship based on mutual trust and cooperation will best serve the interests of the firm and the union.

(4) Responsibility towards Government: It is very essential to ensure that the constitution and operations of the firm are within the legal framework as specified by the government. This legal framework depends upon the nature of ownership of the firm, size of the firm and specific industry within which the firm operates. The government has laid down specific rules, guidelines and norms which are to be followed right from the inception. As a manager ensure that the company is operating well within the legal framework and is fulfilling all its obligations towards the government.

(5) Responsibility towards Society: The company has specific duties towards the society. Providing employment to the local citizen is essential; the surroundings and the people living in the vicinity of the factory and office needs to be taken care of. Firms behave irresponsibly and irrational when they pollute their physical environment by realising harmful smoke and gas into the atmosphere discharging toxic effluents into nearby rivers, lakes or seas and dumping their waste matter in surrounding lands. All the detrimental effects on the environment lead to bad effects on the human health. The government is only now realising the irreparable harm which firms, in pursuit of their business, are causing to the environment and the ecological balance.

Vast forests have been indiscriminately felled by firms in their narrow, single-minded pursuit of profit. This has created an imbalance in the ecology of the area.

Floods have become a recurrent feature in areas which had never been known to be flood-prone. The pattern and extent of rainfall is changing. Rare species of animals, birds and plants have become extinct in the wake of the destruction of their natural habitat.

POINTS TO REMEMBER

- The whole concept of Human Resource Management revolves around the theme of managing relations at the workplace. Since mid 1980's Human Resource Management (HRM) has gained recognition academically and commercially.
- Human Resource Management is a series of decisions that affect the relationship between employees and employers; it affects many aspects and is intended to influence the effectiveness and abilities of employees and employers to achieve their objectives.
- The primary objective of HRM is to ensure the availability of a competent and willing and able work force.

- HRM stands for human resources management, which means the art of managing all aspects of the human work force at a company or organisation.
- HRD is a component of HRM that focuses on nurturing employee's skills. The process of hiring new employees can be long and expensive hence most companies employ the strategy of HRD to promote endurance of employees within the company because through this an employee is likely to progressively scale up the managerial ladder.
- Human Resource Development (HRD) is the framework for helping employees develops their personal and organisational skills, knowledge, and abilities.
- The HR manager creates an infrastructure in the organisation that affects employees, customers, supplier and investors.
- Human resources managers handle personnel decisions, including hiring, position assignment, training, benefits, and compensation.
- The organisation or structure of the Human Resource Department depends upon the size of the enterprise, form of the organisation adopted and the types of the activities to be carried out by the department.
- The internal organisational structure of the HRM department varies widely in different companies, depending upon their size. In small companies the function of the HRM department are limited and restricted. Their maybe two or three people working in the department. In case of large organisation the functions carried out by the HRM department are many and varied.
- The Human Resource Manager leads and directs the HR team to enable them to deliver a comprehensive HR service to the business.

Case Study

State Bank of India is the biggest commercial bank in the country. It has approximately, 6000 branch offices across the country. It has been managing these branches with 20 regional offices located in important places in the country. One of those regional offices is located in Maharashtra.

Mr. Mishra is the Regional Manager of Western Region of Maharashtra and the Singh is the HR manager of western region of Maharashtra. Mr. Puri is working as the chief HR manager at the central office Mumbai. Earlier, the central office used to select candidates for different jobs and allot them to different regions. But the bank has recently decided to decentralise the hiring process and hence asked all the Regional Managers to select their own candidates. Mr. Mishra asked various departmental heads at regional office and branch managers to rewrite job description, job specification, estimate manpower needs to send them directly to him. Mr. Singh has received a letter to this effect in the capacity of head of personnel department in the regional office. Immediately he met Mr. Singh and told him that his job was to prepare job description, job specification, estimate manpower for the entire region and as such, he would be authorised to do all those functions instead of departmental heads at regional office and branch managers. But the regional manager did not accept his request and told Mr. Singh that things would go according to his own instructions. Mr. Singh told the regional manager not to discount his request and restore his positional authority.

Questions:
1. What are the main problems in this case?
2. What should be done to resolve the conflict between the Regional Manager and Regional HR Manager?

Questions for Discussion

1. Explain the concept of HRM. Explain the significance of HRM.
2. Explain the concept of HRD. Explain the significance of HRD.
3. The input, through out of output of HRD is human resources. Discuss.
4. Explain the process of HRM in detail.
5. Explain the process of HRD in detail.
6. What are the functions of HRM manager?
7. Explain the duties and responsibilities of a manager.
8. What are the different objectives of HRM?

Questions From Previous Pune University Examinations

1. Discuss in detail the Development Process of HRM, concept and how it is different from HRD? **(April - 2012)**
2. Explain concept of Human Resource Management and discuss the role of HR Manager in detail. **(Oct. - 2012)**
3. Explain the role of HR Manager in an organisation. State various objectives of Human Resource Management. **(April - 2013)**

Chapter 2...

Trends in HRM

Contents ...

Introduction

    2.1 Change in Labour Workforce

    2.2 Emerging Trends in Human Resource Management (HRM)

    2.3 Knowledge Workers

    2.4 Employee Empowerment

    2.5 Challenges Faced by Human Resource Management

    2.6 Mergers and Acquisitions

    2.7 TQM

    2.8 Downsizing

    2.9 Reengineering

    2.10 Outsourcing

    2.11 Expanding into Global Markets

    2.12 Global Workforce

- Points to Remember
- Questions for Discussion
- Questions from Previous Pune University Examinations

Learning Objectives ...

- To understand the changes in labour force, composition, knowledge workers, empowerment
- To gain knowledge of the challenges facing HRM, strategic issues, mergers and acquisitions
- To learn about TQM, downsizing, reengineering, outsourcing, expanding into global marketing
- To study about global workforce

Introduction

The world of work is changing rapidly. As a part of the organisation, Human Resource Management (HRM) must be prepared to deal with the effects of the changing world of work. For HR managers it means understanding the implications of globalisation, work-force diversity, changing skill requirements, corporate downsizing, continuous improvement initiatives, re-engineering, the contingent workforce, decentralised work sites and employee involvement. In this chapter we will discuss these concepts in detail.

Today's business world has no national boundaries and it has become global. The increase in multinational corporations places new requirements on human resource managers. The HR department needs to ensure that the appropriate mix of employees in terms of knowledge, skills and cultural adaptability is available to handle global assignments. In order to meet this goal, the organisations must train individuals to meet the difficulties of globalisation. The employees must have working knowledge of the language and the culture in terms of values, morals, customs and laws of the host (employer) country.

Human Resource Management (HRM) must also develop mechanisms that will help multicultural individuals to work together. As the background, language, customs or age differences become more prevalent, there are indications that employee conflict will increase. HRM would be required to train the management to be more flexible in its practices. This is because tomorrow's workers will come in different colours, nationalities, races and so on, and managers will be required to change their ways to accommodate the diverse employees. This will necessitate managers to be trained to recognise differences in workers and to appreciate and accept these differences.

2.1 Change in Labour Workforce

The industrial labour is characterised by increased diversity. Workforce of any factory/MNC may comprise of people from different countries. Within the diversity of national origins, there is an even wider diversity of cultures, religions, languages and dialects, educational attainment, skills, values, ages, races, genders and other differentiating variables.

Organisations are becoming increasingly cosmopolitan. A typical organisation is emerging as an amalgam of diverse force in terms of gender, race and ethnicity.

Employees in an organisation come from various socio economic background and the managers must be prepared to deal with the challenges it poses. Diversity brings with it added dimensions to the knowledge and exposure of the workforce.

In spite of this, they work together; they maintain their distinct identities, diverse cultural moorings and separate life styles.

Increased participation of women and the elderly are not the only diversity issues reshaping the labour pool but another factor is multiculturalism. Globalisation has reduced barriers to immigration.

It brings with it new ways of thinking and promotes creativity. This enhances the problem solving capabilities of the managers and hence, increases productivity. The social fabric in these organisations becomes more vibrant and the people become more tolerant to other ways of thinking. It enriches the lives of the employees. Such an organisation will have a good public image and will be able to tap skilled workforce of both genders, from various backgrounds. Today's HR managers must learn to live with these diverse behaviours. Diversity, if properly managed, can increase creativity and innovation in an organisation as well as improve decision making by providing different perspectives on problems.

Organisations that have a record of managing diversity in a positive manner tend to be more flexible and more open minded. The HR systems will be more broad based and less standardised. The managements will be able to overcome resistance to change, as already, change would have become part of the work culture. Managers should be sensitive to diversity issues irrespective of their numerical strength in the organisation. Diversity management has become an important aspect of organisational management. An organisation cannot remain a closed community any more.

People come to organisation with different values, needs and expectations. Workforce diversity requires HR managers to recognise and respond to individual differences to retain and motivate employees. Firms must develop diversity training programmes to help employees overcome their biases in their interaction with people from different backgrounds. Periodic group meetings, collecting and disseminating background information on group members and their special interests, cultural awareness training, programmes to celebrate diversity etc. would be part of such diversity management programmes.

The HR manager has to take care that while managing diversity there is no compromise on issues of compliance with the HR policy, strategy and systems.

Change in Labour Workforce in India

The Indian labour market is of a dynamic nature. Liberalisation and globalisation has created a blend in the labour market especially for the educated people of India. In the past, HRM was considerably simpler because the workforce was noticeably consistent.

Today's workforce comprises people of different gender, age, social class, values, personality characteristics, ethnicity, religion, education, language, physical appearance, marital status, lifestyle, beliefs, ideologies and background characteristics such as geographic origin, tenure with the organisation, and economic status and the list could go on.

Diversity is critically linked to the organisation's strategic direction. Where diversity flourishes, the potential benefits for better creativity and decision making and greater innovation can be accrued to help increase the organisation's competitiveness. One means of achieving that is through the organisation's benefits' package. This includes HRM offerings that fall under the heading of the family friendly organisation. A family friendly organisation is one that has flexible work schedules and provides employee benefits such as child care etc.

In addition to the diversity brought by gender and nationality, HRM must be aware of the age differences that exist in today's workforce. HRM must train people of different age groups, to effectively manage and deal with each other and to respect the diversity and views that each one offers. In situations like these a participative approach seems to work better.

India's labour market is under a vigorous disorder over the past few years. A major change is seen in the labour market of India post liberalisation, privatisation and globalisation.

The ever increasing population has led to lack of jobs in government sector and alluring high packages being offered in multi-national corporations has grabbed attention of general public towards them. Also, a surge of institutes providing professional certificates has widened the job prospects in different fields.

51 per cent of the India's total workforce is self-employed owing to delisting of various public-sector industries, opening doors for privatisation. Repercussion of globalisation can be seen in the form of sprawling Multinational corporations having huge hierarchy i.e. jobs at more levels. Also, segregation of ownership from management has generated more managerial positions and separate departments have been created for managing the vast of operations of these giant enterprises.

Some workforce trends that have surfaced in light of the changes in the make-up of the labour force and the nature of the workforce are employment of women in untraditional jobs, flexible schedules, and more detailed training. Allowing employees to be more involved in making their own schedules seems to be helpful in keeping them. Telecommuting has also become more common so that employees can work from home because this option tends to be very appealing to many workers these days, particularly mothers with young children.

Overall, the workforce has many new challenges to meet. Women with children and disabled workers are a rising number in the labour force. Skills are needed more than ever and therefore so are training and education, which will have to be offered by the employer if there are not enough suitable candidates to hire. Over the years the labour force has changed in many ways and it will continue to do so.

2.2 Emerging Trends in Human Resources Management (HRM)

Human resource management, if we see it from the definition perspective *"is a process of bringing people and organisations together so that the goals of each others are met".*

Seen in a practical situation the above definition is just one side of a coin which has limited HRM involvement. HRM today is a different story, it has changed the way we work, and also it helps an organisation to survive in a recessionary period.

Managing and attracting the human resource in today's time is a very difficult task. The role of HR manager has changed a lot from being protector and screener to the role of Savior who acts as planner and change agent affecting bottom of the pyramid where it is blue collar workers and at the Top and Middle level executives.

The trends in human resource industry are dynamic in nature which contributes towards the achievement of organisation goals. Over the years, highly skilled and knowledge based jobs have increased while low skilled jobs are decreasing. This calls for skill mapping through proper HRM initiatives.

Change is inevitable as is always said and that's what Indian organisations are witnessing in management cultures, systems and working style. Alignment with global companies has forced Indian organisations to accept and incorporate change in everyday life which makes role of HRM all the more important.

Some of the recent changes are as follows:
- The policies of many companies have become people centric, traditionally the policies mainly focused on achievement of organisational goals showing negligence towards the human resource.
- Attracting and retaining of human resource has become difficult as loyalty factor is losing its shine, today HR personnel have to motivate and design healthy career road map to make them stay in the company.
- Human Resource Outsourcing is the new name in the industry to replace the redundant traditional HR department. Many HR outsourcing companies in India are already established and some are coming up to support increasing demand of corporate India.
- With the increase of global job mobility, recruiting competent people is also increasingly becoming difficult, especially in India. Therefore organisations are also required to work out a retention strategy for the existing skilled manpower.

HR managers today are focusing on policies (trust, openness & equality), Motivation, Relations etc. Due to new trends in HR the manager should treat people as resources, reward them equitably and integrate their goals with that of the organisational goals through suitable HR policies. Some of the trends can be seen in:

(A) POLITICAL
- Increased demands for transparency in government and organisations.
- Increasing dispersal of national power.
- Narrowing of gaps in national power between developed and developing nations.
- Increase in the power of non-state actors (businesses, organisations such as the World Bank).

(B) ECONOMIC
- Increased government involvement in economic growth.
- Rapidly increasing national debt to GDP ratios.
- Growth and increasing instability of self-governing wealth funds.
- Increase in state capitalism.

(C) SOCIAL
- International and internal migrations.
- Increased interconnectivity of people, organisations and societies.
- Changing family structure.
- Increasing power of women.
- Aging population.
- Population growth.
- Increasing social freedom.
- Accelerated pace of life.
- Urbanisation

TECHNOLOGICAL
- Pace of technological innovation is increasing.
- Genomics.
- "Digitalisation" of lifestyles and work life.
- Breakthrough or transformative technologies.
- Social, economic and cultural connectivity.

2.3 Knowledge Workers

Every knowledge worker in modern organisation is an "executive" if, by virtue of his position or knowledge, he is responsible for a contribution that materially affects the capacity of the organisation to perform and to obtain results. - **Peter Drucker** in **'The Effective Executive'** (1966)

A knowledge worker is a person that adds value to an organisation by processing existing information to create new information that could be used to define and solve problems.

Examples of knowledge workers include:
- lawyers
- doctors
- diplomats
- law-makers
- software developers
- managers
- bankers.

Knowledge workers,

- use their intellect to convert ideas into products, services or processes.
- are problem solvers rather than production workers.
- use intellectual rather than manual skills to earn a living.

A **knowledge worker** is thus anyone who works for a living at the tasks of planning, acquiring, searching, analysing, organising, storing, programming, distributing, marketing or otherwise contributing to the transformation and commerce of information and those (often the same people) who work at using the knowledge so produced.

This term was first used by Peter Drucker in his 1959 book, 'Landmarks of Tomorrow' who forecast in 1973 that, within two decades, it would become impossible to maintain a middle class lifestyle by working with one's hands. Drucker's perceptive comment signalled that the world we knew was changing. He called the new work that would be required to enter the middle class "knowledge work" and the people who performed it "knowledge workers."

A Knowledge worker (also referred to as an intellectual worker or brain worker) is someone who is employed due to his or her knowledge of a subject matter, rather than their ability to perform manual labour. The defining characteristic of these knowledge workers is the level of their formal education. Thus education and development, and to some degree training, will be the central concern of a knowledge society.

Drucker brought about a new profound respect for the workers in which he believed were assets, rather than liabilities. He taught that knowledgeable workers are the essential ingredients of the modern economy. Central to this philosophy is the view that people are an organisation's most valuable resource and that a manager's job is to prepare them through continuing education, development, and training; in addition to freeing them to perform in networks, rather than placing them in strict hierarchies. (Drucker, Collins, Kotler, Kouzes, Rodin, Rangan, Hesselbein, 2008).

Due to the constant industrial growth globally, there is an increasing need for an academically capable workforce. In direct response to this, Knowledge Workers are now estimated to outnumber all other workers in the globe by at least a four to one margin.

A knowledge worker's benefit to a company could be in the form of developing business intelligence, increasing the value of intellectual capital, gaining insight into customer preferences, or a variety of other important gains in knowledge that aid the business.

The issue of who knowledge workers really are, and what knowledge work entails, however, is still debated.

Mosco and **McKercher** (2007) outline various viewpoints on the matter. They first point to the most narrow and defined definition of knowledge work,: "*the direct manipulation of symbols to create an original knowledge product, or to add obvious value to an existing one*", which limits the definition of knowledge work to mainly creative work.

They then contrast this view of knowledge work with the notably broader view which includes the handling and distribution of information, arguing that workers who play a role in the handling and distribution of information, add real value to the field, despite not necessarily contributing a creative element.

Thirdly, one might consider a definition of knowledge work which includes, "*all workers involved in the chain of producing and distributing knowledge products*", which allows for an incredibly broad and comprehensive categorisation of knowledge workers.

It should thus be recognised that the term "knowledge worker" can be fairly broad in its meaning, and is not always definitive in who it refers to. Knowledge workers spend 38% of their time searching for information. They are also often displaced from their bosses, working in various departments and time zones or from remote sites such as home, offices and airport lounges.

Knowledge workers are employees who have a deep background in education and experience and are considered as people who "think for a living." They include doctors, lawyers, inventors, teachers, nurses, financial analysts and architects.

2.4 Employee Empowerment

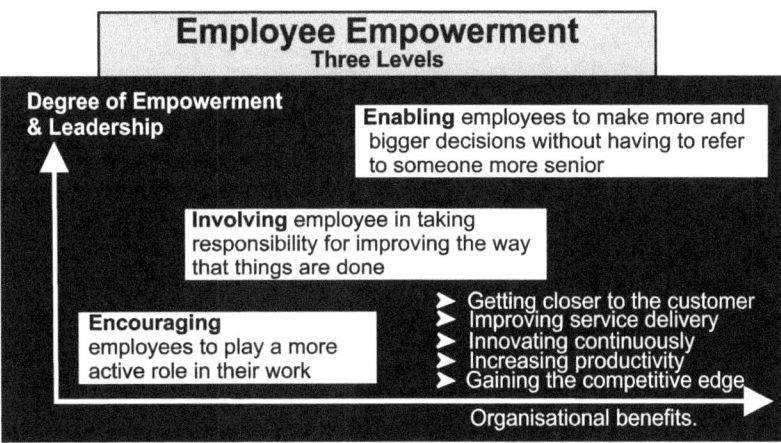

Fig. 2.1: Employee Empowerment

Empowerment is what young job aspirants are looking for in the organisation. More than monetary rewards, it is the feeling that employee owns the job that motivates him or her nowadays.

Empowerment is the process of enhancing the feeling of self-efficacy among the organisational members through the identification of conditions that fosters powerlessness and their removal by both formal organisational practices and informal techniques of providing efficacy information.

Empowered employees are energetic and passionate. They aspire to do better job because they get personally rewarded for doing so.

Employee empowerment is a strategy and philosophy that enables employees to make decisions about their jobs. Employee empowerment helps employees own their work and take responsibility for their results. Employee empowerment helps employees serve customers at the level of the organisation where the customer interface exists.

Employee empowerment is a term that is used to state the ways in which non-managerial staff members can make decisions without consulting their bosses or managers. These decisions can be small or large, depending upon the degree of power with which the company wishes to invest employees.

Employee empowerment can begin with training and converting a whole company to an empowerment model. On the other hand, it might merely mean giving employees the ability to make some decisions on their own.

Empowered employees have an increased sense of ownership in their organisation. Happier than employees in other companies, empowered personnel tend to be more proactive and willing to embrace change. A team full of workers feeling in control of their destinies is far more enthusiastic about their roles and passionate about achievement, which is all good for the company.

Guidelines for Effective Employee Empowerment
- Delegate responsibility along with authority.
- Replace the role of 'managerial parent' with that of 'partner' role.
- Have tolerance for mistakes committed by subordinates.
- Share information with subordinates.
- Allow teams to form. 'Teams' are the best vehicle to empowerment as we always get performance feedback.

For employee empowerment to work successfully some points that need to be kept in mind are:

- **Satisfied Employees**

Employee satisfaction or job satisfaction is, quite simply, how content or satisfied employees are with their jobs. When employees are involved in decision making of the organisation and feel as though they have a choice and can make direct decisions, they sense a greater feeling of self worth. Factors contributing to employee satisfaction include treating employees with respect, providing regular employee recognition, empowering employees, offering above industry-average benefits and compensation, providing employee perks and company activities, and positive management within a success framework of goals, measurements, and expectations.

- **Open Minded Managers**

For employee empowerment to work successfully, the management team must in fact be dedicated in allowing employees to make decisions. Managers might want to define the scope of decisions that their employees can make. Building decision-making teams is often one of the models used in employee empowerment, because it allows for managers and workers to contribute ideas toward directing the company.

Autocratic managers are not able to utilise employee empowerment. These types of managers, who are often called micromanagers, tend to oversee all aspects of their employees' work and usually will not give up control. A manager who is dedicated to employee empowerment must be willing to give up control of some aspects of the business.

- **Encouragement to Employees for their Suggestions**

One easy way for managers to begin empowering their employees is to install suggestion boxes, where workers can place suggestions without fear of punishment or retribution. Simply placing a suggestion box somewhere is only the first step but the Managers must be willing to read and consider the suggestions. In addition, managers can hold meetings where suggestions are addressed.

- **Feedback**

Some suggestions have to be approved for employees to feel that they are having some effect on their company. Failure to approve or implement any suggestions reinforces that all the power belongs to the managers and not the workers. Employee empowerment of any form can work only when managers are willing to be open to new ideas and strategies. If no such willingness exists, the employees are likely to know that they have not been empowered at all.

- **Benefits of Employee Empowerment**

Employee empowerment is a philosophy associated with real benefits for an organisation. Its underlying principle of giving employees the freedom, flexibility, and power to make decisions and solve problems leaves an employee feeling energised, capable, and determined to make the organisation successful. As a result of these management practices, quality of work increases, employee satisfaction increases, collaboration increases, employee productivity rises, and organisational cost decreases.

All of these benefits enable an organisation to achieve a competitive advantage and to encourage its bottom line.

- Many businesses that are looking to improve employee productivity and their overall performance believe that empowering employees will help them achieve this organisational goal.
- Employee empowerment has a positive impact on an organisation's quality of work, employee satisfaction, collaboration, productivity, and costs.
- Organisations that provide employees with the freedom and flexibility to make a difference often see higher quality work from employees.
- Employees in an organisation that focuses on empowerment rate their satisfaction levels as high compared to employees in organisations with a culture that prohibits employee empowerment.
- As employees are empowered and treated as vital components of the organisation, they gain self-confidence and collaborate with others in order to achieve more than one person could by working independently.
- Empowered employees feel a sense of increased responsibility, accountability, and ownership for their work, resulting in increased productivity.
- Empowering employees reduces organisational costs such as employee turnover costs, operational costs, and employee retention costs.
- All of these benefits enable organisations to achieve an extra edge in order to outperform their competitors and to gain market share.

2.5 Challenges Faced by Human Resource Management

The rapidly transforming business landscape means that there are currently many human resource management challenges which will continue to evolve for years to come.

In the face of enormous and rapid changes in the business environment in India backed by liberalisation of economy, globalisation of business, modernisation of technology, large-scale employment, a need exists for a fresh look at the human resources.

Some of the important factors, which may influence the human resources management in future are:

(a) A larger, faster and greater growth of industrialisation is expected in the next decade.

(b) There is possibility for more takeovers, acquisitions and mergers in future in India.

(c) With the presence and influence of more multinational companies as well as higher standards and competitions, there is a possibility for many small indigenous units to become sick.

(d) There is a possibility for the emergence of many large and giant enterprises having economies of scale, forcing the units without the merit of economies of scale and large-scale production to wind up.

(e) ISO 9000 and other international standardisation requirements are bound to dictate higher quality specifications making it difficult for less quality conscious business enterprises to survive.

(f) Large investment and modernisation would require highly skilled and technically trained people who would replace the less-trained, unskilled and redundant workforce.

(g) An increasing number of industrial houses are bound to introduce schemes for golden handshake.

(h) Import of technology may become more common in the days to come resulting in an increasing requirement for highly skilled manpower.

(i) Greater and greater training needs are bound to be identified for updating the technological and behavioural skills.

(j) There would arise greater needs for interpersonal skills, behavioural and counselling skills of executives and hence greater training needs in this direction are bound to rise.

(k) Greater privatisation of business and increase of employment in the private sector may lead to greater training needs in the private sector.

(l) Human resource would gain greater importance by virtue of greater skills and technological expertise and hence human side of the enterprise may gain greater importance.

(m) There would be possibility for change in Government approach to industrial relation policies and HRM approach may receive wide-spread recognition. Even legislations to regulate industrial relations in this direction can be expected.

(n) Greater number of technically and professionally trained manpower may replace untrained or marginally trained executives, technicians and supervisory staff.

(o) Well trained executives and enlightened workforce will expect greater growth prospects, higher remuneration facilities to prove their skill and capability and avenues for participation.

(p) Quality of work-life and quality circle programme may receive greater acceptance.

(q) Computerised information systems will be increasingly used in human resource management and hence effective appraisal system will be in use more and more.

(r) Enlightened management will feel growingly need for human resource approach to deal with their people on account of emerging business environment supported by all the above factors.

With the ongoing changes in Human Resources Management (HRM), it's important that managers, executives and HR employees, specifically, be aware of the challenges that today's HRM team may face. While there are certainly other issues, below given are common to most business or size of company and having policies in place to ensure these challenges are met head-on, so that the workplace becomes more settled and peaceful for everyone.

1. Workplace diversity: This may consist of issues involving age, education, ethnicity, gender, income, marital status, physical limitations, religion, or any number of other things. Understanding the challenges that may be faced by the interaction of any of these diverse groups, as well as the required openness of the company toward such groups, will help HR personnel provide assistance in training employees to work with those they may consider "different," accept that such workers may be present in the business, and agree to treat each other respectfully, even if they never come to agree with each other over various issues.

2. Change management: This is another challenge that more and more HR departments are facing. Being able to deal with their own changing roles in corporate society, in addition to the changes to other jobs, the overlapping responsibilities, and more. Understanding that change is required is the first step toward accepting the change.

3. Compensation and benefits: With a slow economy and tightening corporate purse-strings, the issue of compensation and employee benefits is one that almost every business must deal with. The key is to present mandatory changes in such a way that employees can accept, if not necessarily agree with them while providing non-monetary morale boosting incentives whenever possible to make the changes less traumatic.

4. Recruiting skilled employees: In an era of rising unemployment, it would seem that finding qualified workers would be easier than ever. But that's seldom the case. Many industries are facing dire needs for employees with acceptable skills and the required training or degree. This applies not only to health care, but also to technology and other fields as well, causing many employers to search outside their local marketplace for workers who can do the jobs they need filled.

5. Training and development: This is another challenge that HR managers and personnel must deal with more frequently. With the need to cut training costs, training itself often suffers. Yet the skills an employee needs must still be taught. Many companies are meeting this challenge by providing e-Learning opportunities that allow employees to receive the training they need without the expenses associated with travel, on-site trainers, hours away from their jobs and high-priced materials.

These are only a few of the many challenges an HR department must be prepared to deal with. Knowing in advance what type situation might arise will help the HR personnel to be better equipped in the event that it does. After all, it's always best to hope for the best, but to be prepared for the worst.

2.6 Mergers and Acquisitions

Mergers

Mergers involve the external route to growth, by acquiring firms or parts of firms which they feel would add value to their effectiveness. In merger, one firm loses its identity, whereas in a consolidation both the firms lose their identities to form a new entity. The common practice is to use the term 'merger' to refer to both types of strategies.

A merger is the coming together of two or more firms in which one acquires the assets and liabilities of the other(s) in exchange for stock or cash (consideration), or the firms are dissolved to combine the assets and liabilities and fresh stocks are issued to the shareholders of all the firms. Mergers can be national or across the borders.

Objectives of Mergers

(i) To increase the stock price and/or Price-Earnings (P/E) ratio.
(ii) To develop synergies and thereby improve efficiency and profitability.
(iii) To hike the growth rate.
(iv) To invest funds in a sound business than to use it for profit plough back (internal investments).
(v) To improve the stability of the firm's revenues and sales.
(vi) To have a more balanced or complete product line.
(vii) To diversify the product lines where the present product portfolio is at the peak of the PLC (Product Life Cycle).
(viii) To reduce competition.
(ix) To acquire a needed resource quickly.
(x) To take advantage of tax provisions.

Acquisitions

An acquisition takes place when one company completely buys out another company and the former company remains. Examples include:

- Investment firm buys all the stock of a public company (Blackstone Group buys Harrah's Entertainment)
- Company buys another company (Wachovia buys First Union). If the two companies join together to become a new company, it is then considered a merger (Arcelor and Mittal Steel merge and become ArcelorMittal).

An acquisition or takeover is the buying of one business or company by another company or other business entity. Such purchase may be of 100%, or nearly 100%, of the assets or ownership equity of the acquired entity. Consolidation occurs when two companies combine together to form a new enterprise altogether, and neither of the previous companies remains independently. Acquisitions are divided into "private" and "public" acquisitions, depending on whether the acquiree or merging company (also termed a target) is or is not listed on a public stock market. An additional dimension or categorisation consists of whether an acquisition is friendly or hostile.

Achieving acquisition success has proven to be very difficult, while various studies have shown that 50% of acquisitions were unsuccessful. The acquisition process is very complex, with many dimensions influencing its outcome. "Serial acquirers" appear to be more successful with merger and acquisition (M & A) than companies who only make an acquisition occasionally.

Whether a purchase is perceived as being a "friendly" one or a "hostile" depends significantly on how the proposed acquisition is communicated to and perceived by the target company's board of directors, employees and shareholders. It is normal for M&A deal communications to take place in a so-called "confidentiality bubble" wherein the flow of information is restricted pursuant to confidentiality agreements. In the case of a friendly transaction, the companies cooperate in negotiations; in the case of a hostile deal, the board and/or management of the target is unwilling to be bought or the target's board has no prior knowledge of the offer. Hostile acquisitions can, and often do, ultimately become "friendly", as the acquiror secures endorsement of the transaction from the board of the acquiree company. This usually requires an improvement in the terms of the offer and/or through negotiation.

Acquisition usually refers to a purchase of a smaller firm by a larger one. Sometimes, however, a smaller firm will acquire management control of a larger and/or longer-established company and retain the name of the latter for the post-acquisition combined entity. This is known as a reverse takeover. Another type of acquisition is the reverse merger, a form of transaction that enables a private company to be publicly listed in a relatively short time frame. A reverse merger occurs when a privately held company (often one that has strong prospects and is eager to raise financing) buys a publicly listed shell company, usually one with no business and limited assets.

As an HR things to be avoided and practiced

Things to be Avoided	Things to be Practiced
Ambiguity	Open-minded, flexible and transparent
Selfishness	Greater unity, solidarity for greater cause
Philosophy before merger	New philosophy and shared ideology
Business Practices before merger	Strategic and unified business plans
Dominant behavior	New and shared corporate culture
Self-preservation and internal politics	Equitable, unified and shared decisions
Segmented human capabilities	Enhanced capabilities and trainings
Superior-inferior domain	Equal spirit, motivation and enthusiasm

2.7 TQM

The concept of Total Quality Management (TQM) is of a very recent origin and developed after 1980. It deals with the product in its totality. It is a strategic total approach and comprehensive system of managing the entire organisational activities which result in the production of quality goods and services through constant innovation by doing the right things at the right time. It aims at a continual increase in consumers' satisfaction at continually lower cost. From this point of view, TQM is a continuous process of improvement for all employees and total organisation.

TQM is a very wide concept which encompasses many aspects such as quality management, quality control, quality assurance, quality operations and continuous improvement, etc. In short, TQM means building, controlling and maintaining quality in everything and in every area. It needs collective efforts towards excellence. Quality circles, quality assurance, quality control, quality planning, are some of the important key elements of TQM. TQM is, in essence, a customer-oriented, quality focused management philosophy.

Features or Characteristics of TQM

From the following important features of TQM, we can understand the nature of the concept of TQM properly.

(a) **Continuous Process:** TQM is a continuous process. Constant and continuous efforts are required to improve the quality of goods produced and services rendered and also to reduce costs.

(b) **Quality Management:** Quality management is given importance in TQM approach which helps the organisation to face the challenges from the competitors and to meet the requirements of the customers. Reduction in costs helps to bring in more profits.

(c) **Focus:** In TQM, the focus is on the consumers. Making continuous hard work to satisfy the customers is an integral part of the TQM.

(d) **Defect Free Approach:** In TQM, defect-free approach as an essential part of TQM places emphasis on defect-free work. The idea behind it is to strive for perfection in the work. It definitely helps to improve and maintain the quality of goods.

(e) **People-based Management:** "People-based Management" is one of the principles of TQM. The management has to make its employees understand what they have to do and how they should do. Management should get the feedback about the performance of the employees. Management should make all the efforts to get the co-operation of its employees. If the employees are committed to customer satisfaction, they do their work with responsibility and efficiently. The quality is definitely influenced and improved by continuous involvement of the people working in the organisation. Thus, employees' involvement must be there in the TQM process.

(f) **Reward:** When the management expects their employees to work hard and sincerely, recognition and reward become an integral part of a TQM programme.

(g) **Management by Fact:** "Management by Fact" is another important principle to determine the quality of the product or service that the customers use and what they expect. The present quality level can be used as a benchmark to improve further. Fact-gathering is an essential aspect of continuous improvement. Decisions are taken on the basis of facts.

(h) **Techniques:** In TQM, various techniques such as quality circle, value engineering and quality control etc. are used. It becomes possible to improve systems and procedures through these techniques. Thus, TQM is a very wide concept.

(i) **Responsibility:** TQM, in fact, is the responsibility of the top management. However, the top management cannot do everything alone. Hence, there must be cooperation from the employees working at different levels. Therefore, it requires team-work to make TQM process successful.

(j) **System Approach:** TQM is a systems approach to managing the organisation and business and improving the performance. The systems approach begins with the commitment and effective leadership of top executives and their colleagues.

(k) **Philosophy:** TQM is necessarily a management philosophy which includes all activities through which the needs and expectations of the customers as well as the goals or objectives of the organisation are attained or achieved in the most effective and efficient manner by using the potential of all the employees for the further improvement.

The need and importance of TQM can be understood easily with the help of its advantages :

(a) **Satisfaction of customers:** The customers always expect goods or products of high quality and if they get goods as per their expectation, they are satisfied. In turn, it leads to an increase in the sales of the goods and customer patronage is developed in the market. That is why TQM focuses on the customers' satisfaction.

(b) **TQM helps to face the competition:** TQM concentrates on improvement and maintenance of the quality of the goods. A strict emphasis on TQM helps an enterprise to face competition in the market. The enterprise would become a leader in the market because of properly implemented TQM progamme. It is obvious that because of high quality goods at the lowest possible cost, the enterprise would win the confidence of the customer, capture the market and become the leader.

(c) TQM helps in team-building: In TQM programme, importance is given to creating the right attitude for improving and maintaining the quality of the goods and services and suitable measures are introduced accordingly. Therefore, all the employees in the organisation work as a team which brings an attitude for quality. In turn, it leads to greater involvement and participation of all the employees working in the enterprise and the team of total quality people is developed.

(d) Highly motivated employees: TQM definitely helps to develop a sense of dedication and discipline in the employees. The employees willingly work hard to identify quality developments and waste elimination opportunities. Of course, the employees receive recognition and rewards for their work and services.

(e) Reduction in the complaints of the customers: As TQM attempts to improve and maintain the quality of goods and services for customers' satisfaction, TQM results in less or no customer complaints. In addition, efforts are made to provide goods and services as per the specific needs of the customer. As a result, the customers feel satisfied and there is little need to lodge complaints.

(f) Lower rejection rate: In TQM, defect free approach and just-in-time approach are adopted. As a result, rejection rate decreases and high quality goods are produced. It improves the reputation of the enterprise.

(g) Better facilities to employees: Because of successful TQM programmers, customers feel satisfied and sales increase considerably. The higher profits are utilised to provide better facilities to the employees of the enterprise in terms of training, salary increase, better working conditions, various amenities like transport facilities, recreation facilities, etc. As a result, the employees also feel satisfied.

(h) Chances of expansion and diversification: Because of TQM programme, as the sales and profits increase, it enables an enterprise to expand and diversify. It leads to the growth of the enterprise.

(i) Motivation to the employees: Under TQM, the quality aspect, recognition and rewards motivate the employees of an enterprise to achieve excellence and they accept the philosophy of quality consciousness and strive for better quality of work and product.

(j) TQM is an excellent vehicle to achieve the goals: The most successful TQM programmes are those wherein the quality goals are directly linked to the goals of an enterprise. TQM is goal-oriented and is an excellent vehicle for attaining the important goals of an enterprise i.e. improvement and maintenance of the quality of work and products, increase in sales, consumer-satisfaction, maximising profits and the growth and development of an enterprise.

Thus, TQM is a very important tool in the hands of 'top management' to achieve quality product to develop the human resource and their organisation, to achieve higher productivity and to maximise the profits by expanding markets and increasing the sales.

2.8 Downsizing

Downsizing is a commonly used expression which refers to reducing the overall size and operating costs of a company, most directly through a reduction in the total number of employees.

When the market is tense, downsizing is extremely common, as companies fight to survive in an aggressive climate while competing with other companies in the same sector. For employees, downsizing can be very demoralising and offensive. There are several reasons to engage in downsizing. The primary reason is to make the daily operations of a business more efficient. In general terms, downsizing refers to cutting down of employees in an organisation. It is a crucial step taken by the organisation, when it sees that costs of organisation is going overboard due to excess of employees in the organisation.

In addition, downsizing increases profits by reducing the overall overheads of a business. In other instances, a company may decide to shut down an entire division. In some cases, it becomes apparent that a business has too many employees. This may be because there has been a decline in demand for the company's services, or because a company is running more smoothly and efficiently than it once was. Many offices are heavily bloated with support staff and surplus departments, and these businesses may refer to downsizing as "trimming the fat."

Numerous terms accompany downsizing. Employees may be terminated, fired, laid off, made redundant, or released. A business may be optimised, right sized, or experiencing a reduction in workforce. Some of these terms have different legal meanings depending on where one is in the world; a layoff, for example, may refer to a mass temporary release of employees who will brought back in once business picks up, while a redundant employee is one who is asked to leave permanently. Numerous consulting firms offer assistance with downsizing, often with the use of specialists who visit a business to evaluate it. Since profit is an important bottom line for companies, downsizing measures should be expected by employees, especially when they observe a troubled market or they are working for a struggling company. For employees, the process can be stressful, because they may feel uncertain about whether or not they will continue to be employed. Sometimes, downsizing is very abrupt, with a huge batch of employees being released from employment on the same day, while in other cases it may be a more drawn out and nerve-wracking process in which employees are slowly let go.

Downsizing may prove beneficial in an organisational front but it poses as a major threat in case of employees working in a firm. Downsizing may be due to internal or external changes in an organisation.

Research shows clearly that the human consequences of layoffs are costly and particularly devastating for individuals, their families, and entire communities. While workforce reductions cannot always be avoided, there are compelling reasons why downsizing-related layoffs must be seen as a managerial tool of absolute last option. During an economic downturn a firm must carefully consider its options and assess the feasibility and applicability of cost-reduction alternatives before deciding on layoffs. While a considerable number of research articles that discuss alternatives to downsizing have been published, there is no conceptual understanding of downsizing-related layoffs as they relate to the actual cost-reduction stages of a firm. Indeed, it is critical for an organisation to factor in the concept of cost-reduction and to recognise the specific cost-reduction stage that characterizes the firm's current business position and environment. Thus, a firm needs to determine the expected duration of the business downturn. In order to do so successfully, the executive manager must know exactly where the firm is in its cost-cutting stage. A firm's cost-reduction stage, by definition, refers to the timeframe the company requires to be able to reduce operational expenditures successfully.

If a firm opts for downsizing, it must keep in mind some of the rules of downsizing:

(a) Set targets, deadlines and objectives for downsizing.
(b) Institute a variety of cost cutting procedures, not just head count reduction.
(c) Make clear, direct and emphatic announcements of downsizing strategy.
(d) Give advance notification of downsizing.
(e) Provide all financial benefits agreed upon in time and extend out placement assistance as far as practicable.
(f) Develop trust between management and surviving employees.
(g) Implement downsizing in a fair and humanistic manner.

The fundamental reason to resize the organisation is to improve organisation performance and to reduce costs of operation. Downsizing is a inevitable reality, it is important to do so with dignity and with due consideration to its fallouts from the standpoint of the employer as well as the employee. It is a challenge to the organisation to manage employee exist without disrupting the organisation function.

2.9 Reengineering

"*Business Reengineering is the fundamental rethinking and radical redesign of business processes to achieve dramatic improvements in critical, contemporary measures of performance such as cost, quality, service and speed.*"

Process of Reengineering: The most vital requirement for any successful project is "Communication throughout the organisation."

Step I: Assessing the need for organisational change

The aspects of business that need to be evaluated are:

(a) The current state of the organisation.

(b) The need for change.

(c) Illustrate the desired state.

(d) Communication across the organisation from top to bottom about the change.

   (i) The focus should be on the operating procedures and whether Business Process Reengineering (BPR) is required. It may be possible that significant results can be achieved by TQM, Kaizen and other similar programmes and at a much lesser risk.

   (ii) Normally, the circumstances that initiate a change or ask for BPR are the present way of doing things, what improvements are required and what new circumstances exist in the business environment. Apart from this the other sources of concern for the organisation are the significant advancement of competitor's products and services, whether the demand for your product is dwindling, the political, regulatory and economic environment.

Step II: Identifying the role of all the functional departments for performing Business Process Reengineering

Communication to all levels of personnel is very important from start to finish, to involve everybody and to work towards a common goal. The organisation has to turn to its people to make the change happen. People are the agents of change and are they, who can create the maximum amount of trouble.

The major activities in this step are:

- Establishing a BPR organisational structure.
- Establishing the roles for performing BPR.
- Choosing the right people who will reengineer.

   (i) The most important member of this team is their leader, who has the authority and power to make people follow.

   (ii) The top management should also give substantial support. The job is divided into smaller processes and each process has its own in-charge.

   (iii) The in-charge assesses the performance of the people who actually work on this job.

   (iv) The employees are thus included in the reengineering process and thus resistance by the company personnel to the new process is reduced.

(v) In case of a larger organisation steering committee is constituted who can control the chaos by developing an overall reengineering strategy and by monitoring its progress.

(vi) The reengineering teams can be provided tools, techniques and methods by a specialist or consultant.

Step III: Identifying key performance measures

(a) After having identified the roles of all the functional departments a process is picked which has success potential and which can show success fast.

(b) In many instances, modification in one of the areas like information, IT and people is required.

For example, if a company fulfils orders in six months, while a competitor does the same in two weeks then definitely this process needs reengineering. Thus, one must –

(i) Recognise the change enables,

(ii) Select processes that should be re-engineered,

(iii) Prioritise the selected processes,

(iv) Evaluate pre-existing business strategies,

(v) Consult and know customer's needs and desires, and

(vi) Identify key potential barriers to implementation.

Step IV: Comparing current process with the new objectives

(i) Since, now we know which process to reengineer we should evaluate the present process and compare it with the expected performance. We may not have to check each and every step in this process but we need to understand the underlying reasons for the present performance.

(ii) Further plan the migration from old to new process.

For example, is there a communication gap? is there lack of information?

Thus, the analysis will help us to know where we are and where want to go and further will give an estimate of the current cost, robustness and functional value of each technology that is currently being used.

Step V: Evaluating the impact of change

During this step the actual reengineering begins.

(i) The reengineering team will reveal information about the existing process and ensure that the reengineered process will succeed if implemented.

(ii) A technologist will provide insight as to how a technology can be applied in new and innovative ways.

(iii) The team will now be able to visualise the impact of the changes that are being made.

(iv) Brainstorming sessions of the team will create new process data.

(v) The processes a team identifies for reengineering are sales, purchasing or accounts.

The impact of new technology such as internet, workflow automation, client/server architecture is also evaluated. Internal communication should be increased.

Step VI: Designing the new technology

(i) After having evaluated the various alternatives carefully we are now clear as to what should be our new strategy.

(ii) As such this step will include defining the new technology specifications, describing the new flow of work, the roles of the different people, selecting right people for the right job, describing the new processes, describing detailed technology specifications, technology configurations and their physical specifications.

(iii) New performance measurements, compensation systems, and reward programmes should also be mentioned.

Step VII: Implementation of the transition

(i) An important consideration in this step is the integration of the new process with the other processes.

(ii) If one process is reengineered it must integrate with the other processes. If more than one process is reengineered the new process must integrate with the existing process as well as the newly reengineered processes.

(iii) It is important that impacted staff is included in the transformation process.

(iv) The new organisational structures are established, and training programmes are thus designed.

(v) The staff is educated about the new process and new technology.

(vi) Finally, a structured on-the-job training programme is developed.

Reengineering occurs when more than 70% of the work processes in an organisation are evaluated and altered. It requires organisational members to rethink what work should be done, how it is to be done and how to best implement these decisions. Reengineering changes how organisations do their business and directly affects the employees. Reengineering may leave certain employees frustrated and angry and unconvinced of what to expect. Accordingly, HRM must have mechanisms in place for employees to get appropriate direction of what to do and what to expect as well as assistance in dealing with the conflict that may permeate the organisation. For reengineering to generate its benefits, HRM needs to offer skill training to its employees. Whether it's a new process, a technology enhancement, working in teams, having more decision making authority, or the like, employees would need new skills as a result of the reengineering process.

2.10 Outsourcing

The concept of outsourcing started with Ross Perot when he founded Electronic Data Systems in 1962. EDS would tell a prospective client, "You are familiar with designing, manufacturing and selling furniture, but we're familiar with managing information technology. We can sell you the information technology you need, and you pay us monthly for the service with a minimum commitment of two to ten years."

Outsourcing is contracting with another company or person to do a particular function. Almost every business outsources in some way. An insurance company, for example, might outsource its janitorial and landscaping operations to firms that specialise in those types of work since they are not related to insurance or strategic to the business. The outside firms that are providing the outsourcing services are third-party providers, or as they are more commonly called, service providers.

Although outsourcing has been around as long as work specialty has existed, in current history, companies began employing the outsourcing model to carry out narrow functions, such as payroll, billing and data entry. Those processes could be done more efficiently and therefore more cost-effectively, by other companies with specialised tools and facilities and specially trained personnel.

Currently, outsourcing takes many forms. Organisations still hire service providers to handle distinct business processes, such as benefits management. But some organisations outsource whole operations. The most common forms are information technology outsourcing (ITO) and business process outsourcing (BPO).

Business process outsourcing encompasses call center outsourcing, human resources outsourcing (HRO), finance and accounting outsourcing, and claims processing outsourcing. These outsourcing deals involve multi-year contracts that can run into hundreds of millions of dollars. Frequently, the people performing the work internally for the client firm are transferred and become employees for the service provider. Dominant outsourcing service providers in the information technology outsourcing and business process outsourcing fields include IBM, EDS, CSC, HP, ACS, Accenture and Capgemini.

BPO is the act of transferring some of an organisation's repeated non-core and core business processes to an outside provider to achieve cost reductions while improving service quality. Because the processes are repeated and a long term contract is used, outsourcing goes far beyond the use of consultants. If done well, BPO results in increasing shareholder value. The main difference between BPO and more traditional IT outsourcing is that BPO offers companies a way of achieving transformational outcomes much more quickly. In a typical BPO contract, a service provider takes over a specific corporate function. Effective BPO encompasses much more than just changing who is responsible for performing the process. In BPO, the outside provider not only takes on the responsibility to manage the function or business process, but also re-engineers the way the process has been traditionally done.

Some dexterous companies that are short on time and money, such as start-up software publishers, apply multisourcing using both internal and service provider staff in order to speed up the time to launch. They hire a multitude of outsourcing service providers to handle almost all aspects of a new project, from product design, to software coding, to testing, to localisation, and even to marketing and sales.

The process of outsourcing generally encompasses four stages:
(1) Strategic thinking, to develop the organisation's philosophy about the role of outsourcing in its activities;
(2) Evaluation and selection, to decide on the appropriate outsourcing projects and potential locations for the work to be done and service providers to do it;
(3) Contract development, to work out the legal, pricing and service level agreement (SLA) terms; and
(4) Outsourcing management or governance, to refine the ongoing working relationship between the client and outsourcing service providers.

In all cases, outsourcing success depends on three factors: executive-level support in the client organisation for the outsourcing mission; ample communication to affected employees; and the client's ability to manage its service providers. The outsourcing professionals in charge of the work on both the client and provider sides need a combination of skills in such areas as negotiation, communication, project management, the ability to understand the terms and conditions of the contracts and service level agreements (SLAs), and, above all, the willingness to be flexible as business needs change.

2.11 Expanding into Global Markets

Expanded markets and increased sales mean more profits. Profits mean success for a business. They also mean that a business can make contributions to causes that they believe in.

Globalisation is the increase in international exchange including trade in goods and services as well as exchange of money, information, ideas, and information. It is the growing similarity of laws, rules, norms, values and ideas across countries. Many corporations get their initial exposure to international business when they begin to sell or buy raw materials, goods, or services to or from foreign trading partners. When payments flow in one direction (e.g., an importer making payments to a foreign supplier), the primary need is for foreign exchange or trade finance services. As the company expands its international business, however, it may have the opportunity to set up or acquire operations in a foreign country. Whether this is something as simple as a sales office, or as complicated as a manufacturing subsidiary, the need for international treasury management capabilities truly becomes apparent when an offshore operation both makes and receives payments in a foreign currency. This is when senior management needs to take a hard look at how offshore treasury functions should be integrated with the organisation's domestic treasury management systems.

For many rapidly growing businesses with limited international experience, these global opportunities also present major challenges.

Controlling Expenses

Every business wants to have low expenses; so some companies will therefore enter the global arena to minimise their costs. Companies will examine the resources they need and where they can get them at the lowest price. By searching outside of their own borders, companies hope to find more economical solutions to the production and manufacturing problems they have. Business might choose to take advantage of lower labour costs, they might move manufacturing plants closer to natural resources, invest in new and more efficient technology, or profit from another countries innovations or tax structures.

Diversification

In order to diversify a company's product line they may choose to enter a specific international market. This will apply to both a large scale international business along with a small company.

Companies have a foothold in a number of countries so they don't have to depend on the economy of one country. Companies engaged in international business can protect their investments and their markets by dealing with countries in a variety of countries. A recession in one county won't have a huge effect if business is doing well in another country.

Competitiveness

Many companies expand globally for defensive reasons-to protect themselves from competitors or potential competitors, or to gain advantage over them.

In today's business environment, even a small business is competing with international businesses. A neighbourhood video store is facing competition from a larger international company such as Blockbuster Video. A local store may have a limited selection because of its small size but it may be able to offer more personal service, a more specialised stock or even lower prices. On the other hand, local businesses may find it difficult to compete with the selection and price that multinational companies can offer. If their businesses are too threatened, they may find wider markets or merge with a larger, possibly international company.

2.12 Global Workforce

Global Workforce provides expertise and support to Organisational Missions, Bureaus and other operating units in developing sound workforce development systems that support economic growth and poverty education and increase countries' competitiveness in the global marketplace.

Global Workforce can help to achieve the strategic objectives related to the following Areas of Focus:

(a) Building Workforce Capacity for Increased Competitiveness, Economic Growth and Trade.

(b) Promoting Youth Development and Employment.

(c) Making Education More Relevant to Economic Needs.

(d) Strengthening Partnership and Organisational Capacity for Workforce Development.

(e) Addressing the Workforce Development Needs of Post-Conflict Countries.

(f) Addressing Workforce Impacts of HIV/AIDS.

(g) Building Capacity of Small and Medium Enterprises (SME's) and Promoting Entrepreneurship.

Points to Remember

- A **knowledge worker** is anyone who works for a living at the tasks of planning, acquiring, searching, analysing, organising, storing, programming, distributing, marketing or otherwise contributing to the transformation and commerce of information and those (often the same people) who work at using the knowledge so produced. Examples include lawyers, doctors, software developers

- **Employee empowerment** is a term that is used to state the ways in which non-managerial staff members can make decisions without consulting their bosses or managers. These decisions can be small or large, depending upon the degree of power with which the company wishes to invest employees.

- *Guidelines for Effective Employee Empowerment:*

    (a) Delegate responsibility along with authority.

    (b) Replace the role of 'managerial parent' with that of 'partner' role.

    (c) Have tolerance for mistakes committed by subordinates.

- (d) Share information with subordinates.
- (e) Allow teams to form. 'Teams' are the best vehicle to empowerment. Always get performance feedback.
- The rapidly transforming business landscape means that there are currently many human resource management challenges which will continue to evolve for years to come. In the face of enormous and rapid changes in the business environment in India backed by liberalisation of economy, globalisation of business, modernisation of technology, large-scale employment, a need exists for a fresh look at the human resources.
- With the ongoing changes in Human Resources Management (HRM), it's important that managers, executives and HR employees, specifically, be aware of the challenges that today's HRM team may face. While there are certainly other issues, workplace diversity, change management, compensation and benefits, recruiting skilled employees, Training and development are common to most business or size of company and having policies in place to ensure these challenges are met head-on, so that the workplace becomes more settled and peaceful for everyone.
- These are only a few of the many challenges an HR department must be prepared to deal with. Knowing in advance what type situation might arise will help the HR personnel to be better equipped in the event that it does. After all, it's always best to hope for the best, but to be prepared for the worst.
- Mergers involve the external route to growth, by acquiring firms or parts of firms which they feel would add value to their effectiveness. In merger, one firm loses its identity, whereas in a consolidation both the firms lose their identities to form a new entity.
- An acquisition takes place when one company completely buys out another company and the former company remains.
- **Total Quality Management (TQM)** is a continuous process of improvement for all employees and total organisation.
- **Features or Characteristics of TQM include:** Continuous process, Quality management, Focus, Defect Free Approach, People based management, Reward, Management by Fact, Techniques, Responsibility, System Approach and Philosophy.
- **Downsizing** is a commonly used expression which refers to reducing the overall size and operating costs of a company, most directly through a reduction in the total number of employees

- **Business Reengineering** is the fundamental rethinking and radical redesign of business processes to achieve dramatic improvements in critical, contemporary measures of performance such as cost, quality, service and speed.
- **Outsourcing** is contracting with another company or person to do a particular function.
- Expanded markets and increased sales mean more profits. Profits mean success for a business. They also mean that a business can make contributions to causes that they believe in. Globalisation is the increase in international exchange including trade in goods and services as well as exchange of money, information, ideas, and information
- **Global Workforce** provides expertise and support to Organisational Missions, Bureaus and other operating units in developing sound workforce development systems that support economic growth and poverty education and increase countries' competitiveness in the global marketplace.

Questions for Discussion

1. Explain the Following Concepts:

    (a) Global Workforce, (b) Knowledge Workers
2. What is Employee Empowerment? State its Guidelines.
3. What is Total Quality Management? Explain its Various Features.
4. Explain the Need, Importance and Advantages of Total Quality Management.
5. Describe the various Challenges in HRM.
6. What is Reengineering? Explain its Process.
7. What is Merger? State its Objectives.
8. Explain the concept of Outsourcing.
9. Write short notes on:

    (a) Acquisitions

    (b) BPO

    (c) Downsizing

    (d) Knowledge workers

    (e) Employee Empowerment

Questions from Previous Pune University Examinations

1. Write short notes: **(April - 2012)**
   (a) Employee Empowerment.
   (b) Quality Circles.
   (c) SWOT Analysis.
   (d) Downsizing.

2. Write short note: **(Oct. - 2012)**
   (a) Downsizing.

3. Write short notes: **(April - 2013)**
   (a) TQM
   (b) Re-engineering.

Chapter **3**...

Manpower Planning

Contents ...

Introduction

3.1 Definitions of Manpower Planning

3.2 Objectives of Manpower Planning

3.3 Need for Manpower Planning

3.4 Importance of Manpower Planning

3.5 Short and Long Term Manpower Planning

3.6 Career and Succession Planning

3.7 Recruitment

3.8 Recruitment Procedure

3.9 Selection

3.10 Employment Interview

3.11 Tests

3.12 Induction

- Points to Remember
- Case Study
- Questions for Discussion
- Questions from Previous Pune University Examinations

Learning Objectives ...

➢ To understand objectives, need, importance of manpower planning

➢ To discuss short and long term manpower planning

➢ To gain knowledge of career and succession planning

➢ To study sources of recruitment, procedure, basis of selection, interviews, tests, induction

Introduction

Manpower Planning is putting the right number of people, at the right time, doing the right things for which they are suitable for, and for the achievement of goals of the organisation.

Manpower Planning is also called as Human Resource Planning. Manpower planning is the process of estimating or projecting the number of personnel required for a project (with different skill sets) over a predefined period of time.

It also includes the details like how and when they will be acquired. This whole process is done keeping in view the goals of the organisation.

Manpower Planning is basically considered as a strategy for acquiring, organizing, improving and retaining the human resources of an organisation. Hence, all the efforts are made to have the right type of employees as and when required and to improve their performance in order to make them more efficient, productive and effective when they are engaged on various jobs.

From this point of view, manpower management starts with manpower planning. No doubt, manpower planning is very important function. In this chapter, we will study different aspects relating to manpower planning such as selection and recruitment process, succession planning, etc. Therefore, let us begin with the meaning and few important definitions of manpower planning.

3.1 Definitions of Manpower Planning

- *"Manpower planning is the process including forecasting, developing, implementing and controlling - by which a firm ensures that it has the right number of people and right kind of people, at the right time doing things for which they are economically most suitable".*

  – David A. Decenzo

- According to **E. W. Vetter** human resource planning as *"a process by which an organisation should move from its current manpower position to its desired manpower position. Through planning management strives to have the right number and right kind of people at the right places at the right time, doing things which result in both the organisation and the individual receiving maximum long run benefit".*

- **Coleman** has defined manpower planning as *"the process of determining manpower requirements and the means for meeting those requirements in order to carry out the integrated plan of the organisation."*

- According to **Leon C. Megginson** human resource planning is *"an integrated approach to performing the planning aspects of the personnel function in order to have a sufficient supply of adequately developed and motivated people to perform the duties and tasks required to meet organisations objectives and satisfy the individual needs of goals or organisations numbers."*

- **Lean C. Megginson:** *"Human Resource Planning is an integrated approach to performing the planning aspects of the personnel function in order to have a sufficient supply of adequately developed and motivated people to perform the duties and tasks required to meet organisations objectives and satisfy the individual needs and goals of organisations members".*
- **E. B. Geisler :** *"Manpower planning is the process - including forecasting, developing and controlling – by which a firm ensures that it has the right number of people and the right kind of people, at the right places, at the right time doing work for which they are economically most useful".*
- **Eric W. Vetter:** *"Manpower planning is the process by which management determines how the organisation should move from its current manpower position to its desired manpower position. Through planning, management strives to have right number of and the right kind of people at the right place at the right time, doing things which result in, both the organisations and the individual, receiving maximum long run benefits ".*
- **Coleman:** Human Resource or Manpower Planning is *"the process of determining manpower requirements and the means for meeting those requirements in order to carry out the integrated plan of the organisation".*
- **Strainer:** *Manpower Planning is "strategy for the acquisition, organizing,, improvement and preservation of an enterprise's human resources. It relates to establishing job specifications or the quantitative requirements of jobs determining the number of personnel required and developing sources of manpower".*
- **Gordon Mac Beath:** *"Manpower planning involves two stages. The first stage is concerned with the detailed planning of manpower requirements for all types and levels of employees throughout the period of the plan and the second stage is concerned with Planning of manpower supplies to provide the organisation with the right types of people from all the sources to meet the planned requirements".*
- **James J. Lynch:** *Manpower planning is "The integration of manpower policies, practices and procedures so as to achieve the right number of the right people at the right jobs at the right time".*

Stainer has recommended the following nine strategies for manpower planners:

1. They should collect, maintain and interpret relevant information regarding human resources.
2. They should report from time to time to management regarding the objectives, requirements and existing employees.
3. They should develop procedures and techniques to determine the requirements of different types of manpower over a period of time from the standpoint of organisation objectives.

4. They should develop measures of manpower organising as component of forecasts of manpower requirements along with independent validation.
5. They should employ suitable techniques leading to effective allocation of work with a view to improving manpower.
6. They should develop and employ methods of economic assessment of human resources reflecting its features as income-generator of cost and accordingly improving the quality of decisions affecting the manpower.
7. They should evaluate the prominent, promotion and retention of the effective human resources.
8. They should conduct research to determine the factors hampering the contribution of the individuals and groups to the organisation with a view to modifying or removing these handicaps.
9. They should analyse the dynamic process of recruitment, promotion and loss to the organisation and control these processes with a view to organise individual and group performance without involving high cost.

3.2 Objectives of Manpower Planning

Manpower planning is done systematically and it enables the management to predict the manpower requirements and control the human resources deployed. Due to a more precise matching of manpower needs to the organisation's business plans, it helps to control the wage and salary costs.

It is a systematic effort which comprises five key elements i.e. (1) workforce forecast, (2) proper recruitment and selection of employees, (3) assessment, (4) optimum organisation of human resources employed, (5) future trends affecting the human resources.

From this point of view, manpower planning is basically done with three main objectives – firstly to organise the present human resources completely, secondly to meet successfully the future manpower needs, thirdly to assess and forecast future skills requirements, and finally to provide control measures to ensure that the necessary manpower resources of required quality are available as and when required.

Manpower planning aims to maintain and improve the organisation's ability to attain the objectives by developing strategies purporting to magnify the contribution of human resources.

Dale Yoder suggests certain special objectives of manpower planning which are mentioned below.
1. To establish and to organise the future job requirements.
2. To assure supplies to qualified human resources.
3. To develop available human resources.

4. To organise the current and prospective human resources.
5. To decide sound recruitment and suitable policy.
6. To introduce effective labour cost reduction measures.
7. To recruit and retain the human resource of required quantity and quality.
8. To foresee the employee turnover and make the arrangements for organisation turnover and filling up of consequent vacancies.
9. To fulfil the requirement of expansion, diversification etc.
10. To improve the standards, skills, knowledge, ability etc.
11. To assets the surplus or shortage of human resources.
12. To make the best use of the available human resource.
13. To estimate the cost of human resources.
14. To maintain good industrial relations.

In short, manpower planning is undertaken to achieve the overall objectives of an organisation. There are certain objectives which manpower planning is expected to fulfil. The important objectives are explained below.

1. To use the human resources to the optimum level

Manpower planning should ensure optimum organisation of the human resource currently employed in the organisation. This is expected to be done by providing sufficient work to each employee and by assigning the work according to the skills and abilities of the persons working in the organisation.

2. To provide employees having technical skills to face the changes expected to take place in the future

Constant changes take place in the technological field and accordingly an organisation has to use new techniques in its operation. For this purpose persons who have acquired new skills are needed by the organisation. Manpower planning is carried out with the objective of deciding the skills which will be needed in the future and either training the present employees to acquire the new skills or obtain new employees who possess the new skills.

3. To ensure that the human resources are made available as and when required

Employees are needed in various departments of the organisation which perform different function. They may be needed to fill up the vacancies which arise in the organisation as well as for the additional posts created due to expansion programmes or organisations or diversification programmes. Manpower planning is expected to anticipate the number of employees needed, the kind of employees needed and when they will be needed and make arrangement for supplying the employees from different sources.

4. **To determine the recruitment level and training needs**

   An organisation needs persons to work at different levels. Unskilled, semi-skilled, skilled and highly skilled employees needed by the organisation are recruited in different ways. Manpower planning should decide which category of the employees will be needed and make arrangement for recruitment of the required employees. It is also expected to find out the level of skills and abilities possessed by the present employees and decide what type of training should be given to them to prepare them to face the conditions in the future.

5. **To provide a basis for management and organisation development programmes**

   To face increasing competition and changes which take place in technology and other fields, management has to undertake organisation development programmes and also management development programmes. Manpower planning is expected to provide the basic information by using which such programmes can be prepared and implemented.

6. **To draw attention to trouble spots as far as the human resource is concerned**

   When information about the present employees is studied for the purpose of manpower planning, attention is drawn to those sections or departments where the required types of persons in adequate number are not easily available. Management in such cases becomes aware of the need to take special steps for making good the deficiency. Similarly, manpower planning also brings to the notice of the management those employees who from the organisations point of view are indispensable.

7. **To avoid redundancy and redeployment of the existing employees**

   In the process of manpower planning, it may be found out that in the future the organisation may be required to discontinue the present product line and start production of some new article. Due to this change some jobs which are being done at present may be required to be cancelled and the persons performing these jobs may become redundant. If information about this becomes available well in advance through manpower planning, management can arrange to retrain such employees and redeploy them for the new jobs.

8. **To ensure career planning of every employee and prepare succession programmes for the organisation**

   Manpower planning is not only for the benefit of the organisation but it is also expected to benefit the employees working in the organisation. Employees have expectations of getting opportunities of working at more responsible and higher positions. Manpower planning provides employees not only from outside but also from within the organisation. Posts at higher level may be filled up by promoting the employees working at lower level. Employees are given information about the promotion opportunities and abilities needed for becoming eligible for getting the promotions. Managerial posts are filled up when they becomes vacant by selecting and developing suitable persons from the organisation and for this purpose succession programmes are prepared.

9. To control the costs and increase the productivity of human resources

It is one of the important objectives of the human resource or manpower planning to retain the desired employees longer and keep them functioning more productively and at reasonable cost. Manpower planning attempts to do efforts to reduce labour costs, recruitment and replacement costs. By keeping an inventory of existing human resources in the organisation properly by skills, levels, training, educational qualifications, work experience, salaries and wages, etc. it becomes possible to organise the existing resources more efficiently and productively in relation to job requirements before further manpower additions are made and this leads to control wages and salary costs.

3.3 Need for Manpower Planning

Manpower planning is undertaken to achieve the overall objectives of the organisation as decided by its strategic planning.

Manpower planning is essential to forecast human resources requirements accurately. Manpower planning makes it possible for a company to have a vast pool of qualified people for vacancies that are likely to arise now and also in future.

There is no denying the fact that the continual positive development of a business is owing to its effective planning. Making preparations and arrangements on the basis of what is expected to happen and performing tasks in an organised and capable way is one of the important roles of management in that it involves effective planning process.

It is through the process of planning as well as designing the organisations structure by assigning an assortment of responsibilities to the employees that business organisations may accomplish their set objectives. The concept that the right person should be employed at the right place and at the right time is vitally important to a business as it includes a wide and comprehensive range of activities in relation to the management of man while it entails manpower planning, at the same time, being focused on the effective utilisation of existing human element as well as fulfilling future needs of manpower in the organisations whenever the situations necessitate.

Manpower planning is the process of determining manpower requirements and the means for meeting those requirements in order to carry out the integrated plan of the organisation.

Manpower planning is indispensable for an organisation to perform the activities efficiently as well as in a way that produces desired results. It should be apparent that the organisations development as well as the success of the business is on account of highly competent people that a business organisation keeps.

Manpower planning is one of the key functions of human resource management that manages to maintain the goodwill of a business while giving duly importance to the M (for Men or human element) than that no other M (Machine, Material or Money) is more valuable. It endeavours to the organisations development in totality as well as the success of the business respecting the skills of the employees, their knowledge, experience and talents.

It is concerned with effective recruitment and selection process in order that the skilled workers may be made available each and every time that a business requires. Manpower planning is of great significance for various reasons necessitating the process, at the same time, contributing significantly to the achievement of organisations objectives.

1. To carry on its work, each organisation needs competent staff with the necessary qualifications, skills, knowledge, work experience and aptitude for work.
2. Since employees exit an organisation both naturally (as a result of superannuation) and unnaturally (as a result of resignation), there is an on-going need for hiring replacement staff to augment employee exit. Otherwise, work would be impacted.
3. In order to meet the need for more employees due to organisations growth and expansion, this in turn calls for larger quantities of the same goods and services as well as new goods. This growth could be rapid or gradual depending on the nature of the business, its competitors, its position in the market and the general economy.
4. Often organisations might need to replace the nature of the present workforce as a result of its changing needs, therefore the need to hire new set of employees. To meet the challenge of the changed needs of technology / product/service innovation the existing employees need to be trained or new skill sets induced into the organisation.
5. Manpower planning is also needed in order to identify an organisations need to reduce its workforce. In situations where the organisation is faced with severe revenue and growth limitations it might need to plan well to manage how it will reduce its workforce. Options such as redeployment and outplacement can be planned for and executed properly.

While executed effectively, manpower planning process entails organisation the requirement of present and future vacancies. These situations take place when some employees get retirements, when they are transferred or they are promoted to higher positions.

Similarly, it deals with the situations that arise at the time that employees avail their leaves or in case of their absences. In order that the tasks being assigned may be carried out in a way as has been planned or intended, business organisations need personnel possessing necessary qualifications and experience and that is, to all intents and purposes, accomplished through manpower planning.

In its positive form, it is of great importance to identify the surplus as well as the shortage of the employees so as to move the manpower from one area or activity to another in case of the former, whereas latter indicates providing required personnel. Some of the important tasks concerning the process of manpower planning are manpower demand, supply and manpower audit. It involves organisations total manpower requirement and planning accordingly.

Subsequently, there is a need of manpower supply which is done in both ways, internally and externally. It is needed internally when the employees are transferred or promoted, while the need of external supply arises from the requirement of new workers when a business goes for expansion or changing technology or adopts new methods of production.

In addition, the process entails manpower audit which is carried out through skills inventory. It encompasses detailed information about each employee. It is through this activity that the overall value of an employee to the organisation is determined while it involves organisation the factors such as, which type of workers need to be hired; whether the remuneration is as good as or slightly better or lesser than others.

Adding emphasis on sustaining the skilled workers, manpower audit also analyses the factors that interest the employees to leave the current jobs and move elsewhere in order that the necessary measures may be taken leading to the maximum organising of human resources.

Manpower planning is vital to be in employee's best interests as well as organisations. In addition to undertake proper recruitment methods while implementing appropriate selection procedures for the right candidates and preserving the talents of the employees, it focuses on the requirement and the arrangement of training and development programmes for the employees who need so as to equip them with their jobs requisites and activities.

It is focused on the promotion procedures for those who are skilled and can take challenge of doing more advanced tasks than that are being performed currently. It is by means of manpower planning process that the inefficiencies of the employees are observed that necessary training may be provided, while it maintains morale of the employees.

The process of manpower planning produces the results that improve productivity; the employees may become more efficient and their performance may be more effective. In this way, they can contribute greatly to the total organisation development and the success of a business that depends upon quantity and quality of human resources.

3.4 Importance of Manpower Planning

Manpower planning is related to almost every other personnel function in one way or the other. It serves the goals and objectives to personnel policies and programmes of the organisation. The personnel function of job analysis and performance appraisal make available important inputs for the manpower planning.

Manpower planning is also closely related to those personnel functions whose purpose is to acquire, develop, train and maintain a qualified workforce. In fact, these functions include recruitment, selection, compensation, training and development, career planning, etc. Manpower planning does not anticipate merely the required type and number of employees, but it also helps to determine the action plan for various functions relating to personnel.

Manpower planning is a very important tool and technique of human resource management. It basically aims at maintaining and improving the ability of an organisation to attain the goals of an organisation by developing and organisation properly its human resources. V. S. Narayanrao explained the practical utility and importance of manpower planning in "Manpower Planning Companies" and accordingly –

(1) At the national level, it is generally done by the government and covers various items like population projections, economic development programmes, educational facilities, occupational distribution and growth, industrial and geographical mobility of human resources.

(2) At the sector level, it can be done by the Central and State Governments covering the manpower needs of various sectors such as industry, agriculture, service sector.

(3) At the industry level, it may cover manpower forecast for specific industries e.g. heavy industries, engineering, consumer goods industries, public utility industries, etc.

(4) At the industrial unit level i.e. micro level, it may cover its manpower needs for its various departments and for different types of personnel.

Thus, Manpower Planning plays an important role at micro as well as macro level. It is found today that more complex technologies are functioning in economic, social, business environments. As a result, the organisation face shortages of the right type of human resources. Manpower planning enables to get the right type of personnel in the organisation. Besides this, following points also throw the light on the importance of manpower planning.

(1) Manpower planning involves forecasting of manpower requirements in an organisation and helps the management in anticipating personnel shortages and surpluses and also to develop the ways to avoid or correct problems before they become serious. Further, forecasting of long-range manpower requirements is useful in forecasting the compensation costs involved in that connection.

(2) A proper and systematic forecasting of human resource requirements helps an organisation to determine suitable sources and methods of recruitment. Further, an organisation can also adopt a proper selection procedure depending upon the needs of the jobs. Proper tests can be designed for the purpose of selecting the right candidates for the right jobs. Thus, importance of manpower planning is immense in recruiting and selecting the personnel.

(3) From the view point of training and development, the importance of manpower planning is definitely great. Manpower planning ensures training of employees in an organisation. Training involves imparting of knowledge and developing attitudes, skills, social behaviour, etc. of the employees. Manpower planning identifies the training needs of the personnel of an organisation before hand and then necessary arrangements can be made, training programmes can be chalked accordingly to give the training to the employees. Training helps the organisation to organise its human resources to the optimum. Manpower planning is not only important from the view point of an organisation, but it also helps the employees of an organisation in developing and in application of skills, abilities, knowledge which affect positively their capacity to efficiency, earnings, etc.

(4) So far as performal appraisal is concerned, manpower plays an important role in that area too. Performance appraisal refers to identification of strengths and weaknesses of the employees of an organisation relating to their jobs. It is conducted to know whether the existing human resources possess the necessary qualities and qualifications as per the requirements of the jobs. Manpower planning makes available necessary strategies to correct the weaknesses of the employees by making the proper arrangements for corrective training, retraining, and orientation programmes. As a matter of fact, all these are inter-related activities.

(5) Importance of manpower planning is none-the-less in respect of controlling the labour costs. Efforts are made in manpower planning to assure the timely sufficient supply of labour avoiding the shortages and surpluses of labour which leads to save and control labour costs.

(6) Manpower planning facilitates career development of employees. Career development refers to development of the career of the personnel employed in an organisation. Taking into consideration the long range plans of the organisation, manpower planning can be done. The plans are made known to the employees who can plan their career within the organisation. This leads to further development of employees and motivates them. This role of manpower planning is very important.

(7) An organisation is developed properly when there are better results in the form of higher productivity and efficiency. Manpower planning ensures organisation development from this point of view. If manpower planning is done properly and systematically, problems of low productivity, absenteeism, inter-dependent conflicts, resistance to change, etc. can be tackled and solved efficiently.

(8) Avoiding Disruption in Production: Manpower planning may help the organisation in procuring the skilled and qualified workers because future needs of personnel may be estimated and they are recruited and trained on the basis of a well-developed recruitment and training policy thus lowering the amount of expenditure on training. The production is carried on uninterrupted.

(9) National Policy on Employment: National policy on employment does not permit any employer to oust a worker once recruited by the organisation. Therefore, it is essential to recruit the workers very carefully according to the needs of the enterprise and to develop a recruitment policy of the organisation to avoid any unnecessary hardship in the near future. Only manpower planning can help the organisation in this regard.

(10) Effective Employee Development Programme: No effective employee development programme can be worked out unless it is linked to the manpower requirement of the organisation. While developing the employee development programmes, the talent, abilities and motives of the individuals as well as the organisations objectives in relation to the manpower should be taken into consideration. Only an effective manpower planning can help the organisation make its employee development programmes effective.

(11) Maintaining Good Industrial Relations: An effective manpower planning would help the management in developing good employer-employee relationship. For example, redundancies of workers caused by automation or any other technical change in methods and machines can be estimated well in advance with an effective manpower planning and thus help the management workout the ways and means to avoid the anticipated untoward situation. Management may plan to absorb the redundant workers to some new jobs after proper training. In this manner, an effective manpower planning programme would help maintain better employer-employee relations. Thus, we can say that manpower planning is necessary for the development of the organisation.

3.5 Short and Long Term Manpower Planning

Short term manpower planning refers to staffing needs in the near future. It mainly involves a keen awareness of demand and supply, that is, an awareness of what positions need to be filled and who in the workforce is available to fill those positions. Usually, it is much easier to establish objectives at this point in manpower planning. These objectives usually involve how to attract desirable employees and how to get rid of undesirable ones. Short term manpower planning programmes include recruiting programmes, selection programmes and performance appraisal systems. Assessing the level of success at this point is usually very easy.

The objectives for a period of one year may be considered as a short term manpower planning. The short term objective can be a simple one as procuring an order or project for 25 people. The long term objective may be to start a new industry or to expand the existing market, introduce a new product, develop a new branch etc.

Short term manpower planning can be organised as below:

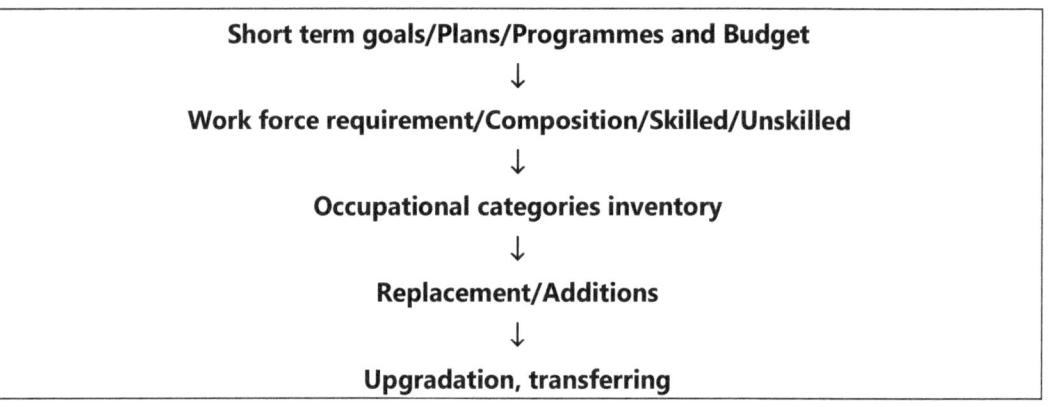

Short term or short range manpower planning is easier to formulate with greater degree of certainty with respect to demand for labour. Authorised expansion is known, adjustment as per technological changes can be implemented. Employees' turnover, Lay-offs and contractual restrictions can be checked. In the case of supply of labours internally departmental, divisional rosters, promotions, expected losers, quits or death needs to be taken care of while externally it fluctuates with the area employment level.

Long term Manpower Planning

Long term manpower planning is becoming one of the most important tasks faced by companies that want to survive. Succession planning is a large part of this type of manpower planning. It involves judging what kinds of skills managers will need in the future and figuring out how to provide people the chance to build these skills. Also, competitive strategy plays a big role in long term manpower planning; will the company want to focus on maintaining innovation or on cutting costs? Career development programmes are often a part of the third phase of this type of planning. The success of long term planning programs is still difficult to assess, but as time passes, more and more information becomes available. Long term manpower planning can be organised as below:

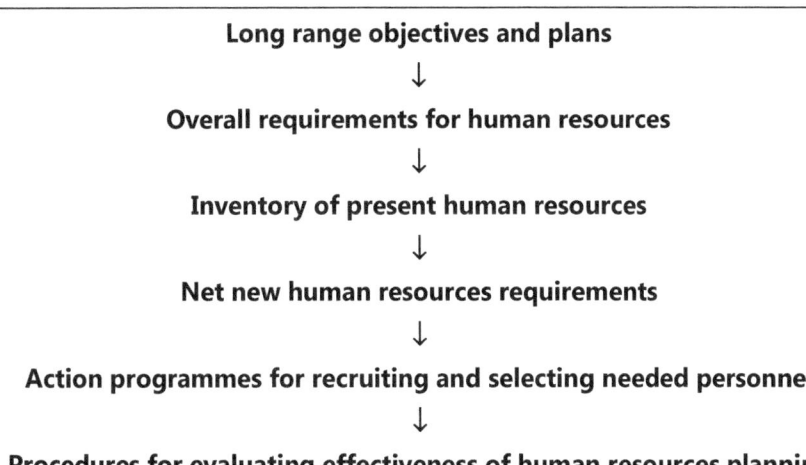

Long term planning is more complicated and is dependent upon mathematical and statistical models as knowledge of demand variables and appropriate measurement techniques. For this two kinds of forecasting techniques exist. Indirect methods involve the forecasting of general rules - production figures. Direct techniques involve the use of methods of estimate labour hours, member of supervisors. Aggregate models are based on several key variables that are known to directly affect the organisation's overall human resource needs. Estimate technique models are used for situations where circumstances make it difficult to use mathematical or statistical approaches.

At the end what matters most for all organisations those that have a high labour turnover must systematically plan their short term and long term manpower needs. These requirements need periodic reviews and are to be adjusted as per changing conditions.

3.6 Career and Succession Planning

Career and Succession Planning is a vital tool for any organisation that wants to retain talented employees and use their potential and skills to increase productivity. This method helps the management to select the most talented lot, train them for further responsibilities and help them succeed to higher positions that have been left vacant by senior personnel. Moreover this system also saves the time and money of the organisation since, there is no need to search for individuals from outside the organisation and waste precious time in conducting interviews.

Through proper career and succession planning, employees can also take charge of their individual careers, experience a sense of security within the organisation and plan a long term association with the company. They know that their performance will be evaluated, recognised and rewarded and their careers will reach great heights within a short span of time. This procedure also helps employees to work harder since they know that they are considered for the next senior position before the organisation thinks of recruiting a candidate from outside.

Some of the key steps involved in a successful career and succession planning are:

- To think strategically and ascertain what type of managers are needed in the future.
- Understand key roles that can bring in more business.
- Identifying the requirements of the key roles and whether any further training is required to fulfil the requirements.
- Identifying the actual talent and potential employees of your organisation who can fill in the required positions or take up responsibilities.
- Identify employees who are going to retire or individuals who are planning to leave.

Career Development

A career is all the jobs that are held progressively during one's working life. Career is progress or course of action a person takes in an organisation. Career includes the specific jobs that a person performs, the kinds of responsibilities and activities that comprise those jobs, movements and transitions between jobs.

Career planning is a process whereby an individual sets career goods and identifies the means to achieve them.

According to **Edwin B. Flippo** *"a career is a sequence of separate but related work activities that provides continuity, order and meaning in a person's life. Career goals are the future positions one strives as part of a career."*

Career planning is a process whereby an individual sets career goals and identifies the means to achieve them. Career planning is the deliberate process by which one selects career goals and the path to achieve those goals. When the organisation intervenes in planning the career, it becomes organisations career planning.

Career development refers to a formal approach used by the firm to ensure that people with proper qualifications and experiences are available when required. Career development steps are those personal movements one undertakes to achieve a personal career plan.

Career management is the process of enabling employees to better understand and develop their skills and interests and use them for the benefit of the organisation and self. Career management is the process of designing and implementing goals, plans and strategies to enable the organisation to satisfy employee needs while allowing or giving freedom to individuals to achieve their career goals though the growth process. Career management activities include opening career development initiatives, providing realistic career-oriented appraisals of posting open jobs.

Career Stages

As we have seen there are various stages in the human life cycle. The same thing can be experienced in career also. To begin with we can have the introduction stage, growth or establishment, maturity or mid stage, decline or retirement. Introduction stage is a career stage that usually ends in one's mid twenties as one begin to switch from college to work.

Growth stage or establishing oneself: It takes pretty long time to find a suitable right job and then to settle down finally with the same job. The problems of this stage include making mistakes, learning from those mistakes and assuming increased responsibilities.

Maturity or mid-career stage: This stage is marked by continuous enhancement is performance, levelling off in performance or the start of declining in performance. Remaining and continuing productive at work is a major challenge. Employees are technically competent and no longer ambitious as they were during the early stage.

Declining or Retiring Stage: The employee enjoys playing a senior person's role. The employee can rest on his credit and gain preference from the youngsters.

Need for Career Planning

1. To attract competent persons and to retain them.
2. To provide suitable promotional opportunities.
3. To enable employees to develop and prepare them to face various challenges.
4. To increase the organisation of managerial talents.
5. To place the right candidate, at the right time in the right place.
6. To reduce employee dissatisfaction and turnover.
7. To promote motivation and morale of the employee.
8. To mutually benefit each other.

Process of Career Planning

1. Analysis of individual skills, knowledge, abilities, aptitudes etc.
2. Evaluation of career opportunities.
3. Evaluation of career demands on the incumbent in terms of skills, knowledge, abilities, aptitude etc.
4. Evaluation in terms of qualifications, experience and training etc.
5. Referring specific jobs to different career opportunities.
6. Setting realistic goals.
7. Preparing career strategy covering areas of change and adjustment.
8. Implementing action plan.

Succession Planning

The goal of succession planning is to identify, develop and make the people ready to occupy higher level jobs as and when they fall vacant. Higher level jobs fall vacant due to different reasons such as promotion, upgradation, death, retirement, resignation, new project etc. Survival, growth maturity and efficient continuous existence of an organisation require a succession plan to fill the various posts.

A succession plan can be for internal employees as well as for external employees. If people are promoted within the organisation then it becomes beneficial to the organisation, since the employee is well informed about the working of the organisation. Organisation can buy the employees' trust and commitment by making them feel that they are part and parcel of the same organisation. The loyalty and belongingness comes when the organisation trusts their organisation employees and confide in them.

Organisation should appraise their employees, identify their needs and requirements and provide them upgradation in the fields required. Employees like to grow and succeed within the organisation. The scope of succession plan grows when there is a steady growth and development for the employees to take up higher responsibilities. Professionally managed organisations keep an eye for able and deserving employees to occupy the new position as and when the need arises.

Advantages of Career Planning

There are many advantages of career planning from the individual point of view and from the organisation's point of view.

(a) Individual Considerations

1. If the employee under the hierarchy chain of the organisation it helps him a lot. The employees understand their own position and the one he wants to achieve in due course of life. The process of planning helps the individual to have proper knowledge of different opportunities available in the organisation.
2. The understanding helps the employee select the career which is suitable to his life styles, preferences, family environment, scope for self-enhancement.
3. It helps the organisation identify the internal employees and upgrade them.
4. Internal promotions, upgradation and deputation motivates the employees, strengthens their morale and also results in increased job satisfaction.
5. Increased job satisfaction enhances employee's commitment and creates a sense of belongingness.
6. Employees will support and wait for their promotions and not switch over the organisation.
7. It improves employee's performance on the job by concentrating and promoting their potential abilities.
8. It leads to employee's satisfaction and happiness.

(b) For Organisations

1. Efficient career planning and development ensures the availability of human resources with required skill and talent.
2. The efficient and proper policies improve the organisation's ability to attract and retain highly skilled and talented employees.

3. A proper career planning ensures that the women and talented people get opportunities for growth and development.
4. The career plans continuously tries to satisfy the expectations and fulfil the needs.
5. Cultural diversity is possible as employees from different cultures helps retaining them. There is unity in diversity.
6. Helping and promoting employee in fulfilling their basic desires helps in increasing the goodwill of the organisation.

Limitations of Career Planning

In spite of planning the career, employees face various problems due to different reasons.

1. **Double income families:** Nowadays, we find nuclear family in most of the places with increase in purchasing power as a resultant of both the members of the family working. Since the husband and wife are working both have to fulfil the responsibilities in the office. At times due to promotions, deputation, transfer and so on. one of the member may have to go to a different place. This may result as a disadvantage for the other partner.
2. **Low ceiling careers:** Some careers do not have scope for much advancement. Employees may not get promotions despite their careers.
3. **Declining career opportunities:** Career opportunities for certain categories reach the declining stage due to the influence of the technological factors.
4. **Downsizing careers:** Business process reengineering, technological changes and business environmental factors force the business firms to restructure the organisations by downsizing. Downsizing results in degrading some employees.

3.7 Recruitment

Recruitment is defined as *a process to discover the sources of manpower to meet the requirements of the staffing schedule and to employ effective measures for attracting that manpower in adequate members to facilitate effective selection of an efficient workforce.*

Today's modern organisations have the value of human capital and its role in their development. Recruitment is the first step in the process of acquiring and retaining human resource for an organisation. Based on the competitive and dynamic business environment, organisations have to quickly assess their staffing requirements and place the right person, at the right time and in the right position. Depending on the organisation's needs, it depends what will be number of people to be recruited and what type of recruitment it will be whether permanent or temporary basis.

- According the **Byers** and **Rue**, "recruitment is *the process of seeking and attracting a pool of people from which qualified candidates for job vacancies can be chosen.*"

- **Edwin B. Flippo** defines the process of recruitment "as *the process of searching for prospective employees and stimulating them to apply for jobs in the organisation.*"
- According to **Denerley** and **Plumblay**, *"recruitment is concerned with engaging the required number of people and measuring their quality."* Thus, it is not only a matter of satisfying the needs of an organisation, but it is also an activity which influences the shape and future of the organisation.

Objectives of Recruitment

1. To attract people with multi-dimensional talents.
2. To induce fresh blood at all levels of the organisation.
3. To promote an organisations culture that attracts competent people to the company.
4. To search for skillful people.
5. To devise methodologies for assessing psychological traits.
6. To design a path that will be based on competence basis and not on a quantum basis.
7. To induct from external environment people who have a vision to lead the company.
8. To reduce the boundaries for inducting new people.

Recruitment means development and maintenance of adequate manpower resource. It means creating a pool of human resource, so that the office organisation can draw from this pool, additional office employees whenever, the need arises. Recruiting is a process whereby the office attracts applicants who have skills and abilities to fill up the job vacancies.

Process of Recruitment

Process of recruitment consists of three sub-systems in recruitment:

(a) Sources of recruitment.
(b) Techniques of recruitment.
(c) Stimulating the candidates.

Sources of Recruitment

In general, the sources of manpower supply can be classified into two broad categories; Internal and External.

There are many organisations which believe that the most consistent source of manpower supply is from within the organisation. It is a good situation to have the source within the organisation. It is a good principle and keeps the morale of the employees high. But there are other sources of manpower supply also which may be used to fill the vacancies in the organisation.

Different sources of recruitment can be employed depending upon factors like the level of the position number of people required etc. Based on the need and required we can check whether we have to select from the internal source or from external source.

Internal Search

In most of the organisations it is a common practice to promote the existing staff to the next level. Organisations try to identify employees from within the organisation, groom them and prepare them to take up higher responsibilities. Many organisations have their HR department doing a very good job. The record the details of all the applications received and keep it in a proper way. They can use their human resource information system for storing and retrieving information about their employees. Vacancies in the organisations are usually placed on notice boards, circulars sent to different departments or through the company's intranet.

Interested candidates may apply in response to such information.

The advantages of internal search are as follows:

1. It helps to understand the organisations hierarchy.
2. It helps in maintaining good employee relations.
3. It helps in understanding the ground level working and get acquainted with the working.
4. It enhances employee morale.
5. It encourages competent and ambitious employees.
6. It embraces the credentials of an individual.
7. Time and money is saved.
8. Return on investment on the workforce is increased.
9. It helps in building a strong, dedicated and motivated team.
10. Good bonding, relationship and trust can be created or developed.
11. Upgradation helps in retaining the employees and reducing the turnover.
12. Good and efficient talent can be selected as we already know the applicant.
13. Reliability, security and sincerity can be achieved from internal source.
14. Promoting from within helps in getting the work done in a faster and easy way.
15. Acceptance from the team is positive.

Disadvantages

1. The organisation may not justify in selecting the right candidate as the decision can be biased.
2. The organisation will suffer of new inventions and system as people who are working are already part and parcel of the same system.

3. Upgradation and competitiveness is not possible.
4. May result into stagnancy.

Internal sources of recruitment include promotion of workers from the lower rank to the upper rank. Majority of companies have established a policy of promotion from within, that is, vacancies other that at the lowest level are filled up by promoting the personnel to the higher offices. Thus, it sets up a chain of promotions that can be filled from those lowest in ranks by giving them training to make them eligible for higher position in the organisation. Such a practice leads to a healthy and progressive atmosphere and lowers the cost of training and the rate of labour turnover. This source of recruitment is generally adopted to fill vacancies of middle and top personnel.

External Sources

An organisation that opts for external recruitment will always have the benefit of getting the select talent that will always come at a cost and time factor. There are various ways and means of recruiting from external sources like advertisements, employee referrals, employment agencies, educational institutions, competitors, walk-in, gate recruitment, internet etc.

Let us begin to understand how the system works in each case.

(a) Advertisements: Advertisements are very effective in recruiting from external sources. The medium of advertisement to be used for depends upon the nature of the job, its level etc. The cost would vary with the status and profile of the vacancy. Many organisations place what is referred to as a blind and wherein the identity of the organisation is hidden. Respondents or applicants are asked to revert back to the post box number or a consulting firm. When the organisation does not wish to publicise the fact that it is seeking to fill an internal position or wants to displace a person it can use a blind advertise. Using television, radio and internet as media for job advertisement is increasing. Employment portals like naukri.com, monster.com, yahoo, Dot jobs domain etc. have become easier and faster.

Most experts are of the opinion that advertisements should contain the following information:

1. The job content, nature of business and size of the organisation.
2. The area and exact location.
3. Job specification and description.
4. Reporting hierarchy and work culture.
5. Benefits-monetary and non-monetary.
6. Job requirements fresh or experienced.
7. Growth prospects and security.

(b) Employee Referrals

Under this method usually the employees who work in the organisation refer their friends and acquaintances for the vacancies in the organisation. Employee referrals are normally used to recruit for lower and middle level management positions. Employee referrals can be a good source of recruitment. When employees recommend successful referrals they are paid monetary benefits.

The advantages of this method are:
1. Generally the employees will refer good candidates.
2. The candidate gets to know about the working structure and responsibility.
3. The employees also feel happy over his contribution.
4. It saves lot of time and money of the organisation.

Disadvantages
1. Employees may refer friends and relatives who are not competent.

(c) Employment Agencies

State agencies: Technicians and fresh graduates registered themselves with these local employment agencies.

Private agencies provide a meeting ground for the organisation and the candidates and simplify the overall recruitment process. They invite applications from interested candidates, scan them for the first round of short listing and finally short list the suitable candidates for the vacant positions in the organisations. Normally the private agencies charge a percentage of the pay package offered. Head hunters normally charge high fees for their services as they do the working for specialised category, specifically for the tap management.

(d) Campus Interviews

Educational institutions offer placement services to their students. The institutions invite some of the best companies to their campus for recruitment. Campus recruitment also helps in building a long-term relationship between companies and educational institutions.

(e) Unsolicited Applications

The candidates who are willing to work for the organisation drop into the company with an application or email their needs. The company does not have any recruitment; hence they collect the information and store it for further need.

(f) Job Fairs

Job fairs are type of campus recruitment in which recruitment process of various institutions is conducted. Participating institutions or an independent institution acts as host. Prospective students may have to pay nominal fees for registering.

(g) Consultancy Firms

In many cases the companies do not conduct the recruitment exercise but they outsourced it to the consultancy firms.

(h) Poaching and Raiding Method

The literal meaning of poaching is to intrude on another's preserves in order to take an undue advantage and raiding means an unauthorised invasion. In poaching and raiding the company following this practice contacts competitor's employees secretly or otherwise woos them to join its force.

Poaching and raiding method is done in indirect way by hiring a consultant. Such a consultant is a specialist in poaching and raiding and keeps records of key employees of different industry sectors. Organisations who want to lead always take the benefit of such things.

(i) Former Employee

Former employees' means individuals who have once worked in the enterprise and were either laid off or have left the organisation for personal reasons and now eager to return. Former employees with a good record may be preferred. These will require less initial training to bring them up to the standard of production than a complete stranger to the enterprise.

(k) Intermediaries

This system of recruitment is most current in Indian industries. Intermediaries are generally known as jobbers, mukaddam, choudary or contractors. Management generally consults these intermediaries at the time of requirement. However, this system of recruitment has led to many abuses.

(l) Recruitment at the Gate

Sometimes, direct recruitment of workers is made at the gate of the factory or office. Generally the number of vacancies, nature of work and time of interview are notified by the personnel department on the notice boards at the gate. Prospective candidates attend the interview at the appointed time and get the appointment. This system of recruitment is generally used to recruit unskilled workers.

(m) Private Agencies

Some private agencies are also doing a great service in recruiting technical and professional personnel. They provide a nationwide service in attempting to match the demand and supply of personnel. Many private agencies tend to organise in a particular type of job like sales, office, engineers, etc.

(n) Professional Bodies

Some professional institutions like institute of company secretary etc., maintain a register of qualified persons from which they recommend the names of the job seekers to the employers when asked for.

(o) Personnel Consultants

Consultants who organise in the recruitment of managers and other sector officials are now being called upon to assist the management in filling of these posts. Companies hire the services of these consultants at the time of recruitment of senior officials. These consultant agencies, on receiving requisition from the client companies advertise job descriptions in leading newspapers and periodicals without disclosing the names of the employers. The applications received are passed on the concerned employers. Sometimes, these firms screen, interview and select the candidates, if asked for by the company.

(p) Trade Union

In some companies trade unions also assist in recruiting the staff. Such a sense of cooperation helps in developing better labour relations. This source of labour supply cannot be relied upon on the ground that sometimes trade unions support a candidate who is not fit for the job and is not acceptable to management. Such view really worsens the labour relations.

(q) Part-time Employees

Sometimes, persons are employed to dispose of the heavy seasonal work or the arrears of work temporarily on part time basis. These part time employees form a good source of labour supply as and when vacancies occur. Vacancies are filled up amongst them if they fulfil the requisite qualifications to suit the jobs.

3.8 Recruitment Procedure

Generally, every organisation has its own recruitment policy. It may vary year to year in the light of changing environments and situations. Recruitment policy assets the objectives of the recruitment and also provides a framework for implementing the recruitment programme in the form of procedure or process. As a matter of fact, recruitment is a process used by an organisation to locate and attract job seekers in order to fill the job positions. An organisation has to choose that recruitment method and sources which produce the best pool of candidates quickly and cost efficiently.

Though the line managers play an important role in the recruitment process, most of the work is actually done by the HR professionals keeping before the following important goals of the recruitment programme.

(a) To attract sufficient number of candidates having suitable qualities and qualifications as per the job requirements,

(b) To achieve cost efficiency,

(c) To adjust and hold employees in the organisation by giving them promotions or transferring them to suitable jobs.

(d) To help in complying with legal provisions.

(e) To create more culturally diverse work force.

(f) To maintain healthy business environment.

Recruitment is called as a process because certain important steps are required to be followed while recruiting the candidates. The three important phases of a recruitment process are as follows:

(1) Planning

(2) Implementation

(3) Evaluation

The recruitment planning procedure can be divided into five steps. Obviously, the first step in recruitment planning procedure is to identify the vacancies. The HRM department has to plan for future openings in the short as well as long-term. Vacancies are created when the present employees retire, or resign or expire and new vacancies are created if an organisation develops. Considering various factors, number of employees to be recruited is found out well in advance.

Once, the vacancies are identified, the decision regarding as to how these vacancies are to be filled in is required to be taken. In this second step, first it is required to be cleared that whether there is a need to find out a new person to fill the vacant position or any other alternative is available i.e. to promote an employee of the organisation. Further, a decision as to whether to go for contingency personnel or core personnel is also required to be taken in this step. Contingency personnel are the workers who are employed by a supplier agency and they work on temporary basis as per terms and conditions. Core personnel consist of employees who are employed as permanent employees. Here again, an organisation has to decide whether to recruit the core personnel internally or externally. It is found that many organisations restrict external recruitment primarily to entry level jobs and jobs above the entry level are filled to enhance the morale and motivation of the employees.

Next step in the process of recruitment planning process is to identify the target population. In this phase, there are two important issues i.e. (1) Specification of worker requirements, and (2) Finding out specific segment in the applicant population. So far as specification of worker requirements is concerned, an organisation has to identify specific requirements of the job wise duties and responsibilities, salary range, competencies needed, experience, educational qualifications, skills and capabilities, etc. In deciding the specific segment in applicant population, attention should be paid as to whether all qualified applicants are to be called or to focus only on certain segments of the qualified applicants. So far as internal recruitment is concerned, it is required to decide whether all qualified employees should be considered or only some highly qualified employees should be considered. In case of external recruitment, it is required to decide as to whether all potential applicants are to be considered or merely target certain types.

After the applicant population is targeted, the next step is to determine how to notify the applicants. We have already studied the methods or techniques of recruitment. Suitable methods such as advertisements, campus interviews, notice boards, etc. for communicating vacancies can be used.

Finally, the most suitable candidates are invited for the interviews and other related assessment procedures. The important goal of the recruitment activity is to attract the right people at the right time for the right jobs. But the task of the manpower managers is not completed on recruiting the employees only. They have constantly to review and improve the methods of recruitment and various sources of manpower supply. Sources for recruiting should be periodically evaluated. For this purpose, various criteria are required to be considered. Any method or source which is very effective at present may not be that effective later on in view of changed environments or situations. Hence, it is necessary to develop a long-range recruiting programme through careful assessment. A sound recruitment programme necessitates proper appraisal of each source of recruitment and each method or technique of recruitment from the view point of the relative qualities of the employees it has provided. Further, recruitment activity must be integrated with the human resources planning of the organisation. As a matter of fact, evaluation involves especially the following three important activities.

(a) Calculation of the number of applicants generated from each recruitment method, source and job success.

(b) Determination of the cost effectiveness of each recruitment method.

(c) In the light of changing situations, the need of re-designing and modifying the process.

If you study carefully the process of recruitment depicted below, you can understand it very easily.

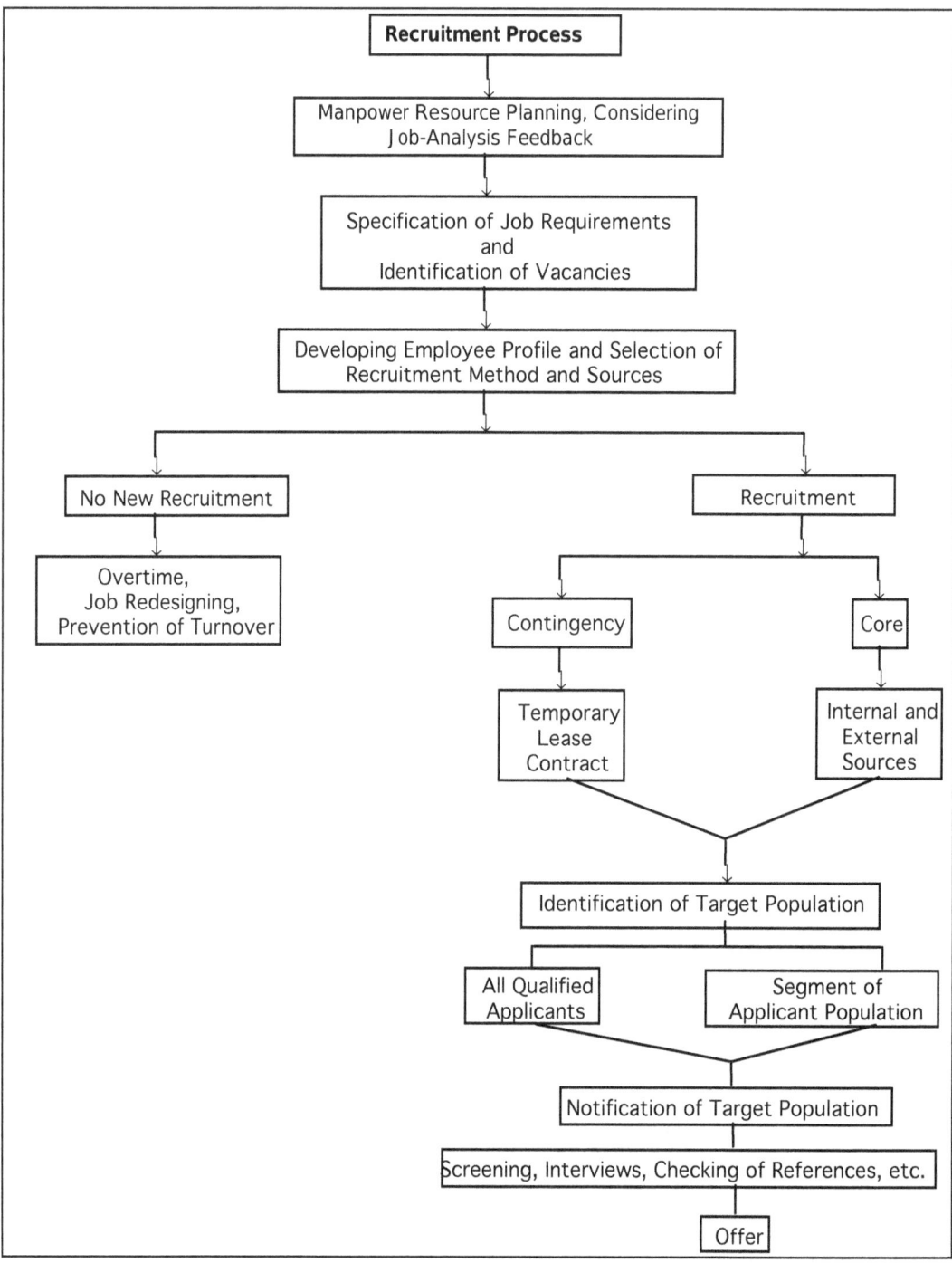

Fig. 3.1: Evaluation of Recruitment Procedure

3.9 Selection

Selection is the process of differentiating between applicants in order to identify those with a greater likelihood of success in a job. Once the potential applicants are identified, the next step is to evaluate their qualifications, qualities, experiences, capabilities, etc. and make a selection. From this point of view, selection refers to the process of offering jobs to the desired applicants.

The selection phase is complicated, lengthy and time consuming. The management has to make necessary efforts to select the people who are fit for the jobs. Selection of candidates implies a scrutiny of candidates to ascertain how far each one measures up to the demands of the job and then a comparison of what each candidate has to offer against the specification of that job and the person needed to fill it. It is matching the candidates the requirements or choosing a right person for the right job.

Selection is that stage in the staffing process in which applicants are divided into two classes i.e. (1) those who will be offered employment, and (2) those who will not be. As more candidates generally are rejected than hired, the selection process is called a rejection process. For this reason, selection process is very often described as a negative process.

Difference between Recruitment and Selection

According to **Edwin B. Flippo,** "*Recruitment is a process of searching for prospective employees and stimulating and encouraging them to apply for jobs in an organisation.* It is often termed positive in that it stimulates people to apply for jobs to increase the hiring ratio; i.e. the number of applicants for a job. Selection on the other hand tends to be negative because it rejects a good number of those who apply, leaving only the best to be hired.

	Recruitment	**Selection**
Objective	To attract maximum number of candidates so that more options are available.	To choose best out of the available candidates.
Process	Creating application pool as large as possible. It is known as positive process.	More and more candidates are shortlisted and rejected. May be one or two are selected. This is known as negative process.
Technique	Recruitment techniques are not very intensive, requiring high skills.	Highly organised techniques are required. In the selection process only personnel with specific skills like expertise in using selection tests, conducting interviews etc. are involved.
Outcome	The outcome of recruitment is application pool which becomes input for selection process.	The outcome of selection process is in the form of finishing candidates who will be offered jobs.

Selection through various techniques that are reliable and proper ensures a better choice of employees. Selection of employees is a very crucial, complex and continuing function. If right employees are selected to perform right jobs, the employee contribution and commitment can reach at the optimum level and employee-employer relations remain congenial. Capable, skilled employees are the valuable asset of an organisation. Systematic and well planned selection helps an organisation to derive certain following advantages which make clear the importance of selection.

(1) It becomes possible for an organisation to build a desirable culture and suitable norms in the organisation through proper selection of newcomers.

(2) The employees get satisfied when they feel that their capabilities, skills, etc. are properly when selection is done through internal sources.

(3) Right candidates in the right place help to increase the productivity, reduce the costs and make their organisation successful. It influences the shape of an organisation's future.

(4) Proper selection facilitates proper placement i.e. fitting the right employee for the right job considering his skills and capabilities. Further, it facilitates training. If newly recruited employees lack in certain areas, suitable training programmes can be organised for them.

(5) Proper selection facilitates optimum use of available resources – both the physical as well as human resources. When proper candidates are selected, various resources are handled and organised properly.

(6) Proper selection makes possible the proper placement. This results in job satisfaction and improved morale of the employees. Employees feel a sense of technology towards their organisation.

(7) Proper selection helps to reduce the employee turnover. When candidates are selected properly, they may get adjusted easily to the new environment in an organisation and hence, do not wish to leave it.

Selection Process

The selection process in an organisation depends on the strategy and objectives of the organisation, the tasks and responsibilities associated with the job, the qualification required, experience and characteristics required to carry out the task and responsibilities, selection process involves a number of steps - Screening of application forms, selection tests, selection interviews, checking of references, physical examination, approval by appropriate authority and handing over the selected candidate for orientation to placement selection. The basic idea in the selection process is to solicit maximum possible information about the candidates to ascertain their suitability for the employment.

The recruitment policy and the job design are determined by the organisations objectives. The selection process begins with the review of applications. These applications can be either in the company's specific format or a general application by the candidate. The candidates may have to undergo a written test, fairly well in the test may permit them to face the interview.

Application Pool from Recruitment Process

Screening of application forms:	Eliminate those not meeting initial criteria.
Selection tests:	Eliminate those below and off point.
Selection interviews:	Eliminate those not meeting job and organisations requirements.
Checking of references:	Eliminate/reconsider those with adverse remarks.
Physical examination:	Eliminate those not meeting physical standards.
Approval by appropriate authority:	Adopt objectivity.
Final selection:	Congratulate.
Employment contract:	Inform about all possible terms and conditions.
Evaluation:	Check the reliability and validity.

Selection Process

The various steps involved in the selection process are as follows

1. **Application Pool:** The basic aim at the recruitment level is to attract more and more applications so that there are more options available at the selection stage.
2. **Screening of Applications:** The real process of selection begins with the screening of applications. Prospective employees have to fill up the applications forms provided by the company or can write an application on their own. Based on the screening of applications, only those candidates are called for further process of selection those who fit in to the organisation standards.
3. **Selection Tests:** Many organisations hold different kinds of selection tests to know more about the candidates or to reject the candidates who cannot be called for interview etc. Selection tests may give information about their aptitude, interest, personality etc. which cannot be known by application forms.
4. **Interview:** Selection tests are normally followed by personal interview of the candidates. The basic idea here is to find out overall suitability of candidates for the jobs, it also provides opportunity to give relevant information about the organisation to the candidate. In many cases, interview of preliminary nature can be conducted before the selection tests.

5. **Checking of References:** Many organisations ask the candidates to provide the names of referees from whom more information about the candidates can be solicited. The visual referees may be previous employers, persons associated with the educational institutions from where the candidates have received elimination.

6. **Physical Examination:** Physical examination is carried out to check the physical standards of fitness of prospective employees. The practice of physical examination varies a great deal both in terms of coverage of timing. Some organisations have general check up of applicants to find the major physical problems which may come in the way of effective discharge of duties.

7. **Approval by Appropriate Authority:** On the basis of the above steps, suitable candidates are recommended for selection by the selection committee. Organisations may designate the various authorities for approval of final selection of candidates for different categories of candidates. Top level manager, board of directors may be the approving authority, for lower levels functional heads may be approving authority.

8. **Find Selection:** After the approval of the competent authority the selection is final and the candidate concerned may be informed accordingly. Sometimes more than one name may be suggested by the selection committee and approved by the competent authority for a single position.

9. **Employment Contract:** The relationship between the organisation and its employees is a contractual one and from this point of view, anyone who is in the employment of the company and draws salary or wage is an employee irrespective of the position held by a person. The implication of contractual relationship is that both employee and organisation must enter into employment contract indicating the various terms and conditions of the employment.

10. **Evaluation:** During the process, evaluation tries to measure the reliability and the validity of various steps used in the selection process. Evaluation measures the outcomes of the selection process in terms of the performance of those who have been selected. Out of the steps of the selection process the first three steps i.e. Screening of application forms, selection tests and interviews - provide maximum information about the candidates on the basis of which selection is generally made.

Selection Procedure

The selection procedure followed by an organisation is tailor made to fit into their needs and requirements. Each organisation has its own set procedure as per the needs and requirements.

Let us discuss the three main factors:

1. Nature of Selection: It depends on the requirements of the organisation. At times the requirement can be for a manual labour. In this case the shop floor manager can decide and select any individual whose meet the requirements. If that selection of a manager is to be done then the procedure will be different. In this case the needs of requirements and the standards are different. So one needs to basically understand the need and requirement in the organisation and accordingly plan for the same. This has to be done in proper way otherwise it may result into heavy expenditure.

2. Policy of the Company: As a practice most of the companies usually short-list more than the actual number needed, with a view to use them at the last stage.

3. Period of Probation: The length of the probation varies from organisation to organisation. Normally the period is of six months or a year. However, if the period is longer than there is uncertainty in the minds of the selected candidate about his future and may not work up to expectations.

Steps in the Selection Procedure

1. Receiving of applications.
2. Application screening a fact finder which helps one in learning about an applicant's background and life history.
3. A properly conducted interview to explore the facts and get an introduction of the applicant and his family details and other relevant information.
4. A physical test helps to explore the health and stamina.
5. To explore the surface area and get an objective look at a candidate's suitability for a job.
6. A referee check.
7. Final selection approval by management and communication of the decision to the candidate.

3.10 Employment Interview

An interview is a procedure designed to get information from a person and to assess his potential for the job he is being considered for on the basis of oral responses by the applicant to oral enquiries by the interviewer. Interviewer has formal in depth communication with the applicant to evaluate his suitability.

It is one of the most important tools in the selection process. This tool is used specially for the top level and middle level category it involves two way exchange of information. The interviewer learns about the applicant and the candidate about his employer.

Objectives of Interviews

1. To obtain additional information about the candidate.

2. Information about the job, company, its policies and procedure, this information is to be provided to the candidate.
3. To evaluate the suitability of the candidate.
4. To find out the period of association.

Types of Interviews
1. Informal interview
2. Unstructured interview
3. Formal interview
4. Planned interview
5. Patterned interview
6. Non-directive interview
7. Depth interview
8. Stress interview
9. Group interview
10. Panel interview

(1) **Informal interview:** It is the interview which can be conducted at any place by any person to secure the basics of non-job related information.

(2) **Unstructured interview:** It is the interview in which the candidate reveals his knowledge on various items/areas, his background, expectations, interest etc.

(3) **Formal interview:** In this type of interview all the formalities, procedures like fixing the value, time, panel of interviewers, opening and closing, intimating the candidates officially.

(4) **Planned interview:** The course of the interview is preplanned and structured depending on job requirements. The questions for discussions are structured and experts are allotted different areas and questions to be asked.

(5) **Patterned interview:** Aims at testing the candidates job knowledge about duties, activities methods of doing the job, critical areas, methods of handling these areas.

(6) **Non-directive interview:** It is the interview in which specific questions may not be asked for but general questions concerning the job, responsibilities, qualities, it can be asked for. Besides job, the information and questions pertaining to hobbies, interest to can be asked for.

(7) **Depth interview:** The candidate would be examined extensively in the core areas of knowledge and skill pertaining to the job. Experts in the relevant field examine the candidates by posing relevant questions as to extract critical answers from the candidate. The candidate can be asked to explain even minute operations of the job performance.

(8) **Stress interview:** It aims at testing the candidate's job behaviour and level of withstanding during the period of stress and strain. Interviewers test the candidate by putting him under stress and strain by interrupting the applicant from answering, criticising his opinions, asking questions pertaining to unrelated areas.

(9) **Group interviews:** All the candidates are brought into one room and are interviewed one by one under this method. This method helps a busy executive to save valuable time and gives a fair account of the objectivity of the interview to the candidates.

(10) **Panel interviews:** A panel of experts interviews each candidate, judges his performance individually and prepares a consolidated judgement based on each expert's judgement and weightage of each factor.

3.11 Tests

The most vital technique of selection which has gained significance in recent years is testing. Employment tests help the management in evaluating the candidate's suitability to the job. Employment test is an instrument designed to measure the nature and degree of one's psychological potentialities, based on psychological factors, essential to perform a given job efficiently. Tests are useful in selection, placement, promotions, performance appraisal and potential appraisal.

Concepts of Testing

1. **Job Analysis:** One of the important testing concepts is job analysis as it provides basic information about the type of the candidate needed by the organisation. Job specification and job requirements provide information about the demand made by a job on the incumbent. Employee specification gives the information about the characteristics, qualities, behaviour of the employee. Employee specification is the basis to decide upon a particular test or tests and minimum acceptable score in order to test whether the candidates possess the required amount of degree of behaviour of qualities like intelligence, aptitude to perform the job successfully.

2. **Reliability** of a test refers to the level of consistency of score obtained throughout a series of measurements. If a candidate obtained same score in the tests conducted in the first, second and third time, under the same conditions, it is said that the test is reliable.

3. **Validity:** Any selection device aims at finding out whether a candidate possess the skills required by a particular job or not. Each selection test aims at finding out whether the candidate has the required proficiency or not. The validity of a test is the degree to which it measures what it is intended to measure. A valid test predicts accurately the level of success or failure of a candidate on the job. According to Dale S. Beach there are five kinds of validity: concurrent validity, predictive validity, content validity, construct validity and face validity.

Types of Tests

There are different types of tests:
1. Aptitude tests
2. Achievement tests
3. Situational tests
4. Interest tests
5. Personality tests

(1) **Aptitude Tests:** These tests measure whether an individual has the capacity to learn a given job if given adequate training. Aptitude test is further divided into general and mental ability or intelligence and specific aptitudes such as mechanical, clerical, manipulative, capacitive etc.

   (a) **Intelligence tests:** These tests in general measure intelligence quotient of a candidate. These test measure capacity for comprehension, vocabulary, picture arrangement and object assembly. Intelligence test includes sample learning, ability, the adaptability test etc.

   (b) **Mechanical aptitude tests:** These tests measure the capacities of spatial organisations, perceptual speed and knowledge of mechanical matter. These tests are useful for selecting apprentices, skilled, mechanical employees, technicians etc.

   (c) **Psychomotor tests:** These tests measure abilities like manual dexterity, motor ability and eye hand coordination of candidates. These tests are useful to select semi-skilled workers or workers for repetitive operations like packing and watch assembly.

   (d) **Clerical aptitude tests:** These tests measure specific capacities involved in office work. Items of this include spelling, computation, comprehension, copying, word measuring and so on.

(2) **Achievement Tests:** These tests are conducted when applicants claim to know something as these tests are concerned with what one has accomplished these tests are divided into job knowledge test and work sample test.

   (a) **Job knowledge test:** Under this test a candidate is tested in the knowledge of a particular job.

   (b) **Work sample test:** Under this test a portion of the actual work is given to the candidate as a test and the candidate is asked to do it.

(3) **Situational Tests:** These tests evaluate a candidate in a similar real life situation in this test the candidate is asked either to cope with the situation or solve critical situations of the job.

- (a) **Group discussions:** This test is administered through group discussions approach to solve a problem under which candidates are observed in the areas of initiating, leading, proposing valuable ideas, conciliating skills, oral communicating skills, coordinating and concluding skills.
- (b) In basket situational test is administered through in basket. The candidate is supplied with actual letters, telephone and telegraphic message, reports and requirements by various officers of the organisation.

(4) **Interest Tests:** These tests are inventories of the likes and dislikes of candidates in relation to work, job, occupations, hobbies and recreational activities. The purpose of this test is to find out whether a candidate is interested or disinterested in the job for which he is a candidate and to find out in which area of the occupation the candidate is interested.

(5) **Personality Tests:** These tests prove deeply to discover clues to an individual's value system, his emotional reactions and maturity and characteristic mood. They are expressed in such traits like self-confidence, tact, distrust, initiative, judgement dominance, impulsiveness, sympathy, integrity, stability and self-confidence.

- (a) **Thematic Apperception Test (TAT):** The candidates are shown a series of pictures and are asked to write a story based on these pictures. This test measures candidate's conceptual, imaginative, projective and interpretive skills.
- (b) **Inkblot Test:** The Rorschach Inkblot test was first described in 1921. The candidates are asked to see the ink-blots and make meaningful concepts out of them. The examiner keeps a record of the responses, time taken, emotional expressions and other incidental behaviours.

(6) **Other Tests:**
- (a) **Cognitive Ability Tests:** These tests measure mathematical and verbal abilities. Popularly known tests of this category include Graduate Record Examination (GRE) and Schematic Aptitude Test (SAT).
- (b) **Polygraph Test** is an instrument that records changes in breathing, blood pressure, pulse and skin response associated with sweating of palms and plots these reactions on paper.

Placement

When the candidate reports to duty, the organisation has to place him initially in that job for which he is selected. The candidate immediately will be trained in various related jobs during the period of probation of training. Probation period generally ranges from six months to one year. If the employee's performance during the probation period is satisfactory he will be placed immediately on a job.

Placement includes initial assignment of new employees and promotion, transfer or demotion of present employees. Placement is the determination of the job to which an accepted candidate is to be assigned and his assignment to that job.

3.12 Induction

Introducing the new employee who is designated as probationer to the job, job location, surroundings, organisation, organisation's surroundings, various employees are the final step of employment process. Some of the companies do not lay emphasis on this function as they view that this function will be automatically performed by the colleagues of the new employees. This process gains more significance as the rate of turnover is high among new employees compared to that among senior employees. This is mainly because of the problems of adjustment of adaptability to the new surroundings and environment.

Induction is essential as the newcomer may feel insecure, shy, nervous and disturbed. This situation leads to instability and turnover. Induction plays important role in acquainting the new employee to the new environment, company rules and regulations.

Induction is *the process of receiving or welcoming an employee when he first joins a company and giving him the basic information he needs to settle down quickly and happily and start working.*

Induction process helps the candidate know:
1. about the company's history, objectives, policies, procedures, rules and regulations, codes etc.
2. about the department.
3. about the superiors, subordinates etc.

About the Company
(a) History, growth, products, market, customers of the company.
(b) Working conditions of employment.
(c) Salary structure etc.
(d) Different types of leave.
(e) Disciplinary rules of procedure.
(f) Grievance procedure.
(g) Career growth, promotions policy.
(h) Education, training and development.
(i) Uniforms etc.

About the Department

The head of the concerned department introduces the new employee to the important employees and describe the working of the department. The superior will then introduce the new employee to all the employees in the section, explain in detail about the job material, machine, equipment with which the worker has to work. He is informed about his position in the department, organisation structure etc.

About the Superiors and Subordinates
- Introduce the new employee to the superior to whom he should report.
- Introduce the new employee to his subordinate with whom he has to work.
- Introduce the new employee to the subordinates who will report to him.

Objectives of Induction
- Putting the new employee at ease.
- Creating interest in his job.
- Providing basic information about the working arrangement.
- Indicating the standard of performance expected.
- Indicating the behaviour expected of him.
- Creating the feeling of social security.
- Department head introduces to all the employees of the department.
- Providing information about the duties, responsibilities, rights, facilities, provisions, welfare measures etc.

POINTS TO REMEMBER

- Manpower Planning is putting the right number of people, at the right time, doing the right things for which they are suitable for, for the achievement of goals of the organisation.
- Manpower Planning is also called as Human Resource Planning.
- Manpower planning aims to maintain and improve the organisation's ability to attain the objectives by developing strategies purporting to magnify the contribution of human resources.
- Manpower planning is essential to forecast human resources requirements accurately. Manpower planning makes it possible for a company to have a vast pool of qualified people for vacancies that are likely to arise now and also in future.
- **Short term manpower planning** refers to staffing needs in the near future. It mainly involves a keen awareness of demand and supply, that is, an awareness of what positions need to be filled and who in the workforce is available to fill those positions.
- **Long term manpower planning** is becoming one of the most important tasks faced by companies that want to survive.
- **Career planning** is a process whereby an individual sets career goals and identifies the means to achieve them. Career planning is the deliberate process by which one selects career goals and the path to achieve those goals.
- The goal of **succession planning** is to identify, develop and make the people ready to occupy higher level jobs as and when they fall vacant.

- **Recruitment** is defined as a process to discover the sources of manpower to meet the requirements of the staffing schedule and to employ effective measures for attracting that manpower in adequate members to facilitate effective selection of an efficient workforce.
- **Selection** is the process of differentiating between applicants in order to identify those with a greater likelihood of success in a job. Once the potential applicants are identified, the next step is to evaluate their qualifications, qualities, experiences, capabilities, etc. and make a selection.
- An **interview** is a procedure designed to get information from a person and to assess his potential for the job he is being considered for on the basis of oral responses by the applicant to oral enquiries by the interviewer. Interviewer has formal in depth communication with the applicant to evaluate his suitability.
- Employment **tests** help the management in evaluating the candidate's suitability to the job. Employment test is an instrument designed to measure the nature and degree of one's psychological potentialities, based on psychological factors, essential to perform a given job efficiently. Tests are useful in selection, placement, promotions, performance appraisal and potential appraisal.
- **Induction** is essential as the newcomer may feel insecure, shy, nervous and disturbed. This situation leads to instability and turnover. Induction plays important role in acquainting the new employee to the new environment, company rules and regulations.

Case Study

Mr. Shrikant is in charge of a factory in Pune, which employs fifteen people, five of whom work in the factory, three of these employees run machines, one supervises and the fifth moves the finished goods by handcar. This fifth position which demands no skill other than driving a handcar, needs to be filled and three applicants have responded.

The first is Mr. Dutta who is forty-five, unmarried and a Navy veteran. Mr. Dutta has a poor work record. During his five years in Lonavala he has worked on seasonal labour and occasional odd jobs, he drove a forklift in the Navy while working at Lonavala. He has a strong build, which could help although the work is generally light.

Mr. Gaikwad age twenty-two came to Pune two years back from Orissa. He has done farm labour for many years and assembly-line for one year. His command over English is poor. He resides with his mother and seems certain to remain in the area for some time. After having run farm equipment, he should have no trouble steering a handcar.

Mr. Rao is a local boy who finished high school five years ago. Subsequently, he got a diploma from a local institute and is currently employed as an assistant is Gati Transport company, Nigdi. His character references are good. Mr. Rao is small, but he seems quick and was track star in high school.

Questions

1. How much consideration should be given to Mr. Dutta with poor work record? Should Mr. Shrikant check to verify it.
2. How important is a command of English to the job? How quickly could Mr. Gaikwad assimilate enough English to be effective?
3. Should Mr. Rao get the job? How heavily should his references be weighed against his inexperience?
4. Who should be hired? Why?

Questions for Discussion

1. What are the methods of staff selection?
2. You are required to hire 10 sales executives to your company. Describe appropriate recruitment, selection and induction methods you would follow.
3. Outline the factors which affect selection decisions in multiple unit organisations.
4. What is testing in selection? Explain its validity and reliability? What are the different types of employment interviews?
5. What is a reference check? Do you agree with the view that reference check has become a mere formality in the selection process?
6. Explain in brief the various selection techniques in general. Outline those selection techniques which are popularly used in India.
7. "Induction is the guided adjustment of employee to the organisation and his work environment." Discuss.

Questions from Previous Pune University Examinations

1. Explain the Concept of Career Planning. How does it facilitate succession Planning? Discuss. **(April - 2012)**
2. What is Recruitment? Explain various Sources of Recruitment in detail. **(Oct. - 2012)**
3. Define the term Manpower Planning. Explain the importance of Career and Succession Planning in Manpower Planning Process. **(Oct. - 2012)**
4. Write short note on: **(Oct. - 2012)**
   (a) Induction.
   (b) Types of Interviews.
5. Explain 'Recruitment'. State various Sources of Recruitment.
6. "Manpower Planning and Career Planning in an Organisation are two sides of the same coin." Discuss.

Chapter 4...

Training and Development

Contents ...

Introduction

- 4.1 Training and Training Needs
- 4.2 Training Calendar
- 4.3 Return on Training and Investments
- 4.4 Systems Approach to Training (SAT)
- 4.5 SAT Evaluation Process
- 4.6 Methods and Types of Training
- 4.7 Performance Appraisal Methods
- 4.8 Merit Rating
- 4.9 Promotion and Transfer
- 4.10 Job Description
- 4.11 Job Evaluation
- 4.12 Job Enlargement
- 4.13 Job Enrichment
- 4.14 Job Rotation
  - Points to Remember
  - Questions for Discussion
  - Questions from Previous Pune University Examinations

Learning Objectives ...

- ➢ To understand training needs, system approach to training, education, training and development, training calendar, return on training and investments
- ➢ To get acquainted with methods and types of training management
- ➢ To learn methods of performance appraisal, merit rating
- ➢ To understand promotion, transfer, job description, job evaluation, job enlargement, job enrichment, job rotation

Introduction

The world of work is changing rapidly. As a part of the organisation, Human Resource Management (HRM) must be prepared to deal with the effects of the changing world of work. For HR managers it means understanding the implications of globalisation, work-force diversity, changing skill requirements, corporate downsizing, continuous improvement initiatives, re-engineering, the contingent workforce, decentralised work sites and employee involvement. In this chapter we will discuss these concepts in detail.

Effective training or development depends on knowing what is required for the individual, the department and the organisation as a whole. With limited budgets and the need for cost-effective solutions, all organisations need to ensure that the resources invested in training are targeted at areas where training and development are needed and a positive return on the investment is guaranteed. Effective TNA (Training Needs Analysis) is particularly vital in today's changing workplace as new technologies and flexible working practices are becoming widespread, leading to corresponding changes in the skills and abilities needed.

Vital prerequisite for any effective training programme or event is analysing what the training needs are. Simply throwing training at individuals may miss priority needs, or even cover areas that are not essential. TNA enables organisations to channel resources into the areas where they will contribute the most to employee development, enhancing morale and organisational performance. TNA is a natural function of appraisal systems and is key requirement for the award of Investors in People.

The analysis of training needs is not a task for specialists alone. Managers today are often responsible for many forms of people management, including the training and development of their team, and should therefore have an understanding of training needs analysis and be able to implement it successfully.

Effective TNA involves systematic planning, analysis and coordination across the organisation, to ensure that organisational priorities are taken into account, that duplication of effort is avoided and economies of scale are achieved. All potential trainees should be included in the process, rather than rely on the subjective evaluation of managers. Ideally, managers should also receive training in the process of TNA itself, to clarify what they are trying to achieve and what their approach should be.

Training makes a very important contribution to the development of the human resources of an organisation and ultimately helps to achieve its goals and objectives. Hence, training needs are to be effectively identified and effectively managed so that the right type of training can be given to the right people at the right time and in the right manner and form.

4.1 Training and Training Needs

Training is the art of doing the job in a correct, effective and efficient manner and it may even be described as *'something which is necessary for everything'*. Training is telling plus showing plus supervising until the desired change is achieved in the skill attitude or behaviour.

(a) In the words of **Michael J. Jucius.** *"The term training is used to indicate only the process by which the aptitudes, skills and abilities of employees to perform specific jobs are increased."*

(b) According to **Edwin B. Filippo** *"Training is the act of increasing the knowledge and skill of an employee for doing a particular job."*

(c) **Littlefield** says that, *"Training is the process of increasing the skills and knowledge of personnel for the purpose of improving individual and organisational performance."*

(d) In the words of **W. H. Leffingwell**, *"Teaching is the imparting of knowledge; training is the development of habits."*

Objectives and Need of Training

The objectives of training can be summarised as under:

(a) To enable the employees do their current job more efficiently and effectively.

(b) To prepare a worker for a higher level job.

(c) To enable the employee to use his skill, knowledge, ability to the fullest extent.

(d) To improve knowledge skill, efficiency of an employee and to obtain the maximum individual development.

(e) To prepare a worker to undertake different jobs, if another person is absent.

(f) To secure the optimum contribution from employee.

Some other definitions are,

(a) According to **Elmer H. Burack and Robert D. Smith**, *"Training is a planned, organised and controlled activity designed to express some aspect or aspects of present job performance. Training is skill oriented and it is usually intended for the short run welfare of the economy (i.e. organisation). Training is also a key ingredient in the motivation of individuals. An untrained, unskilled employee feels very insecure, lacking the self-confidence necessary for comfortable group relations".*

(b) **Prof. Milkovich and Prof. Boudreau** stated the definition of training as, *"Training is a systematic process of changing the behaviour, knowledge, and/or motivation of present employees to improve the match between employee characteristics and employment requirements".*

(c) According to **Prof. Arun Monappa and Prof. Mirza Saiyadain**, *"Training refers to the teaching and learning activities carried on for the primary purpose of helping members of an organisation to acquire and apply the knowledge, skills, abilities and attitudes needed by the organisation"*. They further opined that *"broadly speaking, training is the act of increasing the knowledge and skill of an employee for doing a particular job"*.

(d) According to **Prof. A. M. Sharma** *"Training may be defined as any organisationally planned effort to change the behaviour or attitudes of employees so that they can perform jobs on acceptable standards. Training provides knowledge and skills required to perform the job"*.

(e) **Prof. C. B. Mamoria** defined the concept of training as *"A process of learning a sequence of programmed behaviour. It is an application of knowledge"*. He further made it clear that *training gives people an awareness of the rules and procedures to guide their behaviour and attempts to improve their performance on the current job or prepare them for an intended job.*

Training needs analysis involves:

- monitoring current performance using techniques such as observation, interviews and questionnaires.
- anticipating future shortfalls or problems.
- identifying the type and level of training required and analysing how this can best be provided.

Training needs can be sorted broadly into three types:

- those you can anticipate.
- those that arise from monitoring.
- those which result from unexpected problems.

Training is given to the employees in order:

(i) To enhance the existing knowledge, skills and abilities, performance capabilities of the employees and to acquire new skills, abilities, knowledge for improving their qualities.

(ii) To increase efficiency and productivity of the employees.

(iii) To help an organisation to fulfill its future personnel needs.

(iv) To improve health and safety of employees.

(v) To prevent wastages, wear and tear obsolescence etc.

(vi) To improve organisational climate.

(vii) To help employees achieve personal growth and development.

(viii) To improve morale of employees.

(ix) To keep abreast of (i.e. up to date with) developments in technical and management fields and also to inculcate a sense of appreciation for other functional areas and an understanding of the linkage of their activities with other areas.

(x) To induct new employees into the organisation.

(xi) To minimise the resistance to change.

Training activity is not an isolated exercise but is an integral part of the total management development activities of an organisation. Therefore, considering the goals and requirements of an organisation, identification of training needs is required to be done. Identification of training needs is a continuous process which involves identification of areas, where employees lack skills, knowledge, abilities etc. in effectively performing their jobs and also identifying organisational constraints, problems which create roadblocks in the performance. Many a time, the need to train personnel is felt when a gap between the present performance of employees and the desired performance is considerably widened. Prof. Price rightly pointed out that, training needs exist when there is a gap between the present performance of an employee or a group of employees and the desired performance. This gap can be ascertained by doing skill-analysis.

Skill-analysis includes the following aspects:

(a) Determination and analysis of various requirements required to perform specific jobs;

(b) Finding out the activities and tasks required to be accomplished for meeting job requirements;

(c) Understanding the procedures and processes needed to accomplish each of the job requirements;

(d) Understanding and analysis of the knowledge, skills and abilities required to accomplish the procedures and processes;

(e) Identification of special problems, if any, in relation to the job and proper analysis of any specific skill, ability required to solve problems.

Training helps organisations in many ways. Because of proper training given to employees, their skills, abilities, aptitudes and attitudes, efficiency and productivity etc. increase. Besides that, various problems relating to production, workers relations can also be solved by analysing the problems and identifying the training needs.

Training needs can be assessed by observation of job performance, surveys, tests, interviews, organisation analysis, performance appraisal etc. There are various techniques which are used to determine training needs.

The **Research Committee of the American Society of Training** has suggested certain techniques for determining training needs which are as follows:

(a) Observations (b) Interviews (c) Group conferences (d) Management requests (e) Questionnaire surveys (f) Examination and tests (g) Performance ratings (h) Personnel records (i) Business and production reports (j) Long-range organisational planning (k) Job analysis.

McGhee and **Thayer** have proposed a model of training needs identification which has the following three components:

(i) **Organisational Analysis:** Organisational analysis involves a comprehensive study and analysis of organisational structure, goals, procedure, process of decision-making etc. If it is done properly, deficiencies can be identified and mechanisms which would be needed to make adjustments in the areas of those deficiencies can be introduced. While doing the analysis, it is studied whether an organisation possesses adequate number of people to accomplish its objectives, goals etc. and whether the persons working with an organisation possess required skills, abilities, knowledge etc. Based on the findings, training needs can be identified properly.

(ii) **Task Analysis:** In identifying training needs, task analysis is considered as an important aspect. Task analysis involves systematic and detailed analysis of various components of jobs which indicates whether the nature of the jobs is changed over a period of time and whether the employees have adequate skills and abilities to perform the jobs.

(iii) **Man Analysis:** Man analysis is more complicated than the two components i.e. organisational analysis and task analysis because of the uncertainty in the behaviour of human beings. While undertaking man analysis, more importance is given to the skills, abilities, aptitude, attitudes, knowledge etc. of the employees and personal records relating to behaviour, absenteeism, production done, regularity etc. are also used.

The importance of training is immense to the employees both from the view point of development and growth of their organisations and themselves. Training helps to bridge the gap between standard performance and actual performance. It attempts to improve current or future performance of employees by increasing their abilities and skills to perform through learning and also by changing their attitudes and aptitudes. Thus, the importance of training in the performance management process is definitely more and moreover, it is found today that training plays a key role in the performance management process.

Training and development of human resources is important to organisations as it helps to increase productivity, heighten morale, reduce the costs and increase organisational stability. Training is also beneficial to the employees as it serves as an important means for the development of effective and productive habits amongst them which help them to improve job performance.

From the discussion done so far, the objectives and importance of training can be stated together in the following way:

Training, may be of any type or kind, should have as its basic objective to improve the behaviour, skills, abilities of the employees so that their performance becomes more productive and useful for them as well as for their organisation. There can be concentration on giving or improving operative skills, interpersonal skills, decision-making skills or more such other skills which help them to achieve various strategic goals.

4.2 Training Calendar

Training calendars are best suited for repeatable and regular demand, such as refresher skills training for infrequently performed technical tasks and for new recruits joining the organisation. In these cases review of what training is required on a regular basis and a look at what new recruits need to be proficient at, soon after they join any organisation is done. Generally, one should consult the management team by checking off which off the following areas needs to be included in the training calendar:

- management
- leadership, and
- supervision skills
- health and safety
- business skills
- skills such as telephone etiquette and inventory management

A typical training calendar might look like this:

Month	Course	Dates	Duration	Area	Venue
February	Certificate IV in Public Safety	1 - 9	7 Days	Thomton	Strategic Corporate Training
February	Certificate IV in Training and Assessment	1 - 9	7 Days	Mudgee	To be advised
February	Certificate IV in Training and Assessment	8 - 16	7 Days	Taree	To be advised
February	TAA Workplace Assessor Course	10 - 12	3 Days	Thomton	Strategic Corporate Training
February	Certificate IV in Occupational Health and Safety	15 - 19	5 Days	Thomton	Strategic Corporate Training
February	Certificate IV in Occupational Health and Safety	17 - 23	5 Days	Taree	To be advised

... (Contd.)

Month	Course	Dates	Duration	Area	Venue
February	Certificate IV in Training and Assessment	22 - 2	7 Days	Thornton	Strategic Corporate Training
March	Certificate IV in Training and Assessment	1 - 9	7 Days	Albury	Greenwell's Fly Fishing Club
March	Conduct an OHS Audit	4 - 5	2 Days	Thornton	Strategic Corporate Training
March	OHS Consultation - Workcover NSW	8 - 11	4 Days	Thornton	Strategic Corporate Training
March	Certificate IV in Occupational Health and Safety	8 - 12	5 Days	Mudgee	To be advised
March	Mining Supervisors Course G2, S2, S3	15 - 16	4 Days	Thornton	Strategic Coprorate Training
March	Certificate IV in Occupational Health and Safety	22 - 26	5 Days	Albury	Greenwell's Fly Fishing Club
March	Certificate IV in Occupational Health and Safety	22 - 26	5 Days	Thornton	Strategic Corporate Training

Fig 4.1: Training calendar

4.3 Return on Training and Investments

Company management wants to know that the money they are spending on training is well spent. They want to know that they are getting a sufficient Return on Investment (ROI). Improvement factors include increased productivity, reduction of waste and improved employee retention.

Measurement of training ROI starts with defining the reasons and goals for the training, determining how much the training costs and verifying the amount of return.

Questions you may have include:
- What is the reason for the training?
- What is the investment in training?
- How is the return measured?
- A company may provide training to their workers, managers, customers, and sometimes suppliers. The ultimate reason for training them should be to improve the profits and repeat business of the company. It is preferred that this improvement is measurable, so that an effective ROI can be determined.

Reasons to train workers
- The reason to train workers and managers is so they will learn to do their jobs better or perhaps learn new skills or technologies that can be applied to the company's goals. Sometimes workers and managers are trained to satisfy government requirements, to ensure safety, or to prevent lawsuits or other forms of company loss.
- Managers are often trained in people-handling skills. Also, companies may allow workers to take training simply as a way to keep them happy in their jobs.

Reasons to train customers and suppliers
- The reason to train customers is so they will understand how to use the company's products effectively. This can prevent problems and expensive service calls.
- Likewise, companies may train their suppliers on the proper method to provide specialised items. This is to ensure the company gets the highest quality parts and supplies needed to make their product.
- Training customers and suppliers follows the Total Quality Management (TQM) philosophy of doing business.

Investment in training
- In order to train personnel, customers or suppliers, a company must pay for the development of training material and the time spent by the trainers in the classroom. This is either absorbed through an in-house training department, paid to outside training companies, or a combination of the two.
- Costs include paying for time off from work, paying trainers, and travel and lodging expenses.

Time spent by workers
- Workers and managers must often take time off from work to attend training classes. Not only is the company paying wages for no work done, but it may also lose opportunities for more sales or productivity during the absence of the personnel. For off-site training, the company may also have to pay for travel and lodging.
- The burdened hourly rate, estimated loss of productivity, and training expenses must be calculated.

Classes for customers
- Classes must also be set up to train customers and suppliers. Training personnel, equipment, and location expenses must be paid by the company, although in some situations the customers or suppliers may pay for their own training.

Keep track of costs
- Obviously, if a company wants to determine their Return on Investment (ROI) for training, they must account for all the money spent, especially the hidden expenses.

Measuring the ROI

- The greatest factor in measuring the Return on Investment (ROI) for training is the definition of what the training is to achieve. Measuring the amount of money generated by a group before and after the training, and then comparing that improvement with the cost of the training is the way to measure the ROI.

If no measurable goals

- Very often there are no specific or measurable goals to achieve for a training session. This is especially true in many of the "soft skills" taught to managers. It is very difficult to measure the results of a manager style training seminar. In fact, the goal for such training might be something like: "To be a better manager."
- If there is no way to measure the effectiveness of the training, the company might be better off simply giving the people money to go on a vacation.

Having specific goals

- If the goal is to improve the productivity of a worker in a certain process, a metric must be determined that leads to a company bottom line number. Before and after training measurements must be made to determine the effectiveness of the training sessions. Then the costs involved in training the personnel can be compared with the real improvement of profits to determine its ROI.
- For example, safety training has a specific goal of reducing the accident rate. Statistics can be made that will verify the effectiveness of such training.

ROI in training customers

- A good way to tell the effectiveness of training customers is the reduction in service calls. The cost of maintaining a service call staff and making repairs can be compared with the cost of training the customers.
- Some companies use service calls as a method for generating revenue. This is an extremely short-sighted way of making money. A quality product that the customer knows how to use will generate repeat business. If the customer must make service calls or send the product in for repairs, that customer may buy from a competitor the next time around.
- Likewise, the return from training suppliers can be measured through the improvement in quality of the goods and services they provide. This will result in the measurable reduction of problems and improved quality of the end product.

4.4 Systems Approach to Training (SAT)

The Systems Approach to Training (SAT) methodology, is a *proven results driven method of training an audience that incorporates evaluation and focused course curriculum development for a specific need, expectation and audience.* The Systems Approach to Training (SAT) methodology is a five-phase process that ensures that training accomplishes the following goal:

A practical, results-oriented training programme that provides people with the skills and the knowledge to do their tasks correctly, efficiently, and with confidence.

Overview

The systematic approach and development model goes by many names; however, Systems Approach to Training has remained the standard. This model takes into consideration audience characteristics, the nature of the knowledge, skills, job, and tasks to be learned, and environmental constraints.

Instructional System Development (ISD) is a field that takes many of its concepts and principles from various disciplines. For example, as an applied discipline, SAT uses learning theory from psychology to determine how a person learns (learning style) and how to best address their learning need. Instructional theory uses that person's learning style to determine how to best design instruction.

The five-phases of the SAT model are:
- Analysis
- Design
- Development
- Implementation
- Evaluation or Control

Metrics may be pictorially represented as a linear model, but the approach involves continuous iterations. Decisions made in one phase affect actions and plans in other phases.

The Systems Approach to Training (SAT) Methodology and the Instructional System Development (ISD) are Synonymous

4.5 SAT EVALUATION PROCESS

Analysis

An aggressive evaluation process to determine the effectiveness of the training programme along with concise customer feedback to ensure that expectations are being met (according to the Training Needs Assessment) is vital for the success of any training programme.

Analysis provides a method of responding to changes in human resource requirements, solving job performance problems, and learning from "real world" experience.

In the analysis phase, detailed practical studies are performed to determine what areas require instruction, learner characteristics, the cost effectiveness of a selected delivery system (e.g. Technology Based Training - TBT), and the scope, timeline, and budget of a training project/programme.

Facts and metrics are gathered to make informed training development decisions and provide the linkage between the job and the training project/programme.

The following types of analysis may be completed:
- Needs or Performance Analysis
- Audience or Learner Analysis
- Job/Task Analysis
- Skill/Knowledge (Ability) Analysis
- Content Analysis
- Learning Analysis
- Instructional Analysis

Design

Design uses the performance information collected earlier to help the training project/programme take shape.

The information gathered specifies, measurable terms, the knowledge, skills, and aptitudes that training will develop learning objectives are developed for groups of related knowledge and skills.

These written statements of learning outcomes define exactly when, what, and how well the learner must perform during training. Defining how individual tasks are performed focuses training development efforts.

In addition, the information gathered permits more effective decisions regarding such things as:
- How the learning materials will be organised and presented
- Learning activities and instructional strategies
- Time spent on each topic
- The use of presentation media
- How learners will be evaluated
- Evaluation instruments

Practical measures as well as written/knowledge tests are produced to ensure that learning objectives are achieved and competencies are reliably evaluated.

Development

Development organises the instructional materials needed for learners to achieve the learning objectives.

Emphasis is on maximising the use of existing materials and resources. Instructor and learner activities are defined and these activities describe how the instructor and learners will perform during training to achieve the learning objectives.

Existing, suitable training materials and lesson plans are selected and new ones produced as needed. Resulting training materials are reviewed for technical accuracy, tried out with a group of learners, and revised if necessary. Performance based training materials are the products of this phase.

Implementation

Implementation is the process of putting the training project/programme into operation. This finalised training is ready to be delivered to the target audience.

If the training is to be instructor-led or facilitated, instructors are selected and trained usually with a train-the-trainer session. Training is delivered as planned and the trainee and the trainer performances are evaluated.

These evaluations serve two purposes:
- First, they verify that the trainees have achieved the learning objectives.
- Second, learner evaluation results and trainer comments are useful for future programme revisions and iterations and follow-up evaluation.

Evaluation or Control

The Evaluation or Control phase ensures training's continuing ability to produce qualified workers.

A Follow-up evaluation is conducted to get an assessment of how well the training prepared the trainees to perform their jobs after having been on the job for a selected period of time.

Evaluation is the dynamic process of assessing performance, identifying concerns, and initiating corrective actions.

Data sources for evaluation often include:
- Exams or Testing
- Surveys
- Phone or Personal Interviews
- Course evaluation results
- Service or product data
- Observations

The systematic approach to training provides a method for analysing, designing, developing, implementing, and evaluating cost-effective, results oriented training programmes.

4.5.1 Meaning of 'Education' and 'Development'

Training is the act of increasing the knowledge and skill of an employee for doing a particular job. Thus, training is imparting knowledge guidance so as to develop the job skills among the operative staff. Development provides wider exposure to management personnel and makes them capable of facing organisational problem and challenges boldly. Training is provided by the superior/foreman and supervisory staff. Development programmes of management are executed by the top level managers and specially invited experts. Training is related to a specific job and is for a short period. Development is general in nature and wide in scope. Development is a continuous process for updating the knowledge of the executives.

Training is given off and on. Initially, it is given if required and thereafter, it is given when transfer is made by promotion, or at the time of introduction of a new technology. Development is a continuous process. It is for refreshing information, knowledge and skills of the executives. Under training, On-the-Job methods are used extensively. In the case of development, off the job methods are used along with on the job methods. Training is not costly since internal methods are used and it is of short duration or period. Development is costly.

Education, training, development are related terms and they differ in nature and orientation. **Education** is basically confined to theoretical learning and gaining knowledge about a subject or subjects in different areas. Education comes first and then training. No training programme is possible and complete without preliminary and formal education. Thus, it can be said that some sort of education is a pre-condition of training.

The Dictionary meaning of the word **'development'** is "causing something to grow". From the view point of training and development of employees, development can be defined as a process by means of which an employee attempts to attain overall improvement in ability, competence, efficiency, etc. thus making progress towards maturity and actualisation of overall personality. Development is a related process and it does not merely cover those activities which improve job performance but also covers all those activities which bring about the growth of the personality so that the employees improve their overall qualities. Development gives more stress on knowledge. Generally, it is understood that development is not primarily skills-oriented. It is a long-term educational process which provides general knowledge and attitudes that help the employees to get to higher positions. Developmental programmes are generally meant for employees in higher positions or those who have been identified as having potential to reach higher positions.

4.5.2 Relationship between 'Education', 'Training' and 'Development'

Education, training and development are correlated terms or concepts. **Education** is the process of acquiring background and basic knowledge of a subject and it is person-oriented rather than job-oriented. Education is common to all employees. **Training** is concerned with the acquisition of knowledge as well as skills that can be applied to perform work of a particular type. It is a process of imparting specific skills. While **development** is a course of action designed to gain knowledge and to create attitudes amongst the employees to realise their potential for growth in their organisation. Development is related to future, more senior jobs or positions rather than present ones. Training an employee or an individual for a higher, bigger and more responsible job means engaging him in 'development'.

4.5.3 Difference between 'Training' and 'Development'

Though training and development include training of employees to perform their jobs efficiently and effectively, there is some difference between training and development.

Training is any organisational planned effort to affect or change the behaviour, attitudes etc. of employees so that they can perform their jobs efficiently on acceptable standards. It provides knowledge, skills etc. required to perform the job. It can be said that training is a process by means of which the aptitudes, skills, capabilities, efficiency etc. of the employees to perform their jobs are increased. Development is also viewed similarly but with more stress on communicating organisational norms, values for the given roles. Development is also a process which helps employees to attain overall improvement in ability and competence and it helps to progress towards maturity and actualisation of personality. Thus, it can be said that training is meant for learning technical operations which provides specific job related information, while development makes clear theoretical conceptual ideas and provides general knowledge and helps an individual to enhance level of understanding various aspects.

Training is a short-term process in which generally non-managerial personnel learn technical aspects, skills and get technical knowledge for definite purposes utilising a systematic and organised procedure. Development is a long-term educational process in which managerial personnel especially learn conceptual and theoretical knowledge useful for management and organisation utilising a systematic, well-planned and organised procedure. Moreover, in developing human resources, the training and development functions are combined properly for developing various skills, abilities and basic attitudes and aptitudes, which lead to personal development and growth. It is considered that for many jobs, proper training is very essential to keep abreast of current developments and to raise the performance abilities of human resources even beyond acceptable levels. Therefore, now-a-days, it is accepted that training and development programmes play a major role in organisational development by changing attitudes and behaviour of the personnel.

4.6 Methods and Types of Training

There are various methods of training. The choice of the methods depends upon several factors like cost of training, number of workers, depth of knowledge required, background of the trainees, purpose of training and so on.

The various training methods may be grouped as below:

(A) On-the-job method
(B) Vestibule training method
(C) Classroom method
(D) Apprenticeship training method

The second and third methods are also known as off-the job training:

(A) On-the-Job Training

On-the-job training as the name suggests is imparted on the job and at the work place where the employee is expected to perform his duties. It enables the worker to get training under the same working conditions and environment and with the same materials, machines and equipments that he will be using ultimately after completing the training. This is the most effective method of training the operative personnel and generally used in most of the industrial undertakings. Under this method, the responsibility to impart training to workers is given to the immediate supervisor who knows exactly what is to be taught to the trainee for better performance or to some outside instructor who is specialist in the field. Under this method the following systems may be included:

(a) Training by Supervisor: Supervisor in-charge is responsible for the training of the operative staff under this system. The supervisor supervises and instructs the employee while on work. Sometimes, he even demonstrates the system of working to the employee. This enables the supervisor and the employee to understand each other better.

(b) Under-study System: Under this system, a senior and experienced workman is assigned the job of teaching the new employee as his under-study. The trainee under this system loses his motivation and morale if the person under whom he is working does not take interest in him. A common version of such training is the three position plan. Under this a man learns from the man above him and teaches the one below him. This system is more suitable in circumstances where the trainer requires an assistant.

(c) Position Rotation: Under this system, the employee is periodically rotated from one job to another instead of sticking to one job just to acquire the general background and knowledge of the functioning of the job. Its major objective is to broaden the background of the trainee in various positions of the job.

(B) Vestibule Training

Under this method, the training is not given on the job but workers are trained on specific jobs in a special part of the plant by models. Training is given in a class room where working conditions are created which is similar to the actual workshop conditions. After training, the worker is put on similar jobs in the workshop. It should be noted that a well qualified and trained instructor should be in-charge of the programme. This method is expensive because there is duplication of material, equipment and conditions found in a real work place but it is a correct blending of theory and practical work.

(C) Class Room Training

Where concepts, attitudes, theories and problem solving abilities are to be learnt, the classroom instruction is the most useful device. In other words it is more associated with knowledge rather than skill. Orientation about organisation, safety training or refresher training can be accomplished most effectively in the classroom. There may be different methods of instruction such as:

(a) **Formal Lecture:** Where depth of theoretical knowledge (such as safety, health, etc.) is required, formal lectures are arranged by the organisation and delivered by the lecturer presumed to be a master of the subject at hand. The lecture method may be used for large groups and therefore cost per trainee is low. Trainees should be permitted to ask questions. Lecturer can also make use of the following other techniques.

(b) **Conference and Seminar:** There are two types of seminar. The first is that, in which a student gives a lecture on some predetermined topic and is followed by discussion and exchange of views under a chairman who sum up the discussion by his fruitful advice and comments. The second method is where all students participate in the seminar under a chairman who sparked off the idea and discussion follows, which in turn, leads to further ideas.

(c) **Case Study:** In case study, a practical problem faced by an industrial unit is discussed at large in the group, possibly to find an optimum solution. The trainee studies the problem and finds the solution. The supervisor reviews the solutions and discusses it with the trainees.

(d) **Role-Playing:** Under this system the trainees play their assigned role (such as the role of supervisor, instructor etc.) under an instructor who prepares them to assign different roles for the play. The above systems in classroom method are not of much value for the operative staff. These are used generally to train employees for various executive positions.

(D) Apprenticeship Training

Apprenticeship training programme tends towards more education than on-the-job training or vestibule schools, in that knowledge and skill in doing a craft or a series of related jobs are involved. The Governments of various countries have passed laws and made it obligatory on the part of the employer (public or private) to provide apprenticeship training. This may be combined with on-the-job training and or classroom instruction. The apprentices get stipend during the training period and are generally offered jobs after the completion of training by the employer.

4.7 Performance Appraisal Methods

Definitions

It is a systematic evaluation of an individual with respect to performance on the job and individual's potential for development.

Formal System, Reasons and Measures of Future Performance

"It is a formal, structured system of measuring, evaluating job related behaviours and outcomes to discover reasons of performance and how to perform effectively in future so that employee, organisation and society all benefits."

Performance Appraisal is the assessment of individual's performance in a systematic way. It is a developmental tool used for all round development of the employee and the organisation. The performance is measured against such factors as job knowledge, quality and quantity of output, initiative, leadership abilities, supervision, dependability, co-operation, judgement, versatility and health. Assessment should be confined to past as well as potential performance also. The second definition is more focused on behaviours as a part of assessment because behaviours do affect job results.

Objectives/Use of Performance Appraisals

1. Promotions
2. Confirmations
3. Training and Development
4. Compensation reviews
5. Competency building
6. Improve communication
7. Evaluation of HR Programmes
8. Feedback and Grievances

Goals of Performance Appraisals

General Goals	Specific Goals
Developmental Use	Individual needs
	Performance feedback
	Transfers and Placements
	Strengths and Development needs
Administrative Decisions / Uses	Salary
	Promotion
	Retention / Termination
	Recognition
	Lay offs
	Poor Performers identification
Organisational Maintenance	HR Planning
	Training Needs
	Organisational Goal achievements
	Goal Identification
	HR Systems Evaluation
	Reinforcement of organisational needs
Documentation	Validation Research
	For HR Decisions
	Legal Requirements

Performance Appraisal Process

1. Objectives definition of appraisal
2. Job expectations establishment
3. Design an appraisal programme
4. Appraise the performance
5. Performance interviews
6. Use data for appropriate purposes
7. Identify opportunities variables
8. Using social processes, physical processes, human and computer assistance

Difference between Traditional and Modern (Systems) Approach to Appraisals

Categories	Traditional Appraisals	Modern, Systems Appraisals
Guiding Values	Individualistic, Control oriented, Documentary	Systematic, Developmental, Problem solving
Leadership Styles	Directional, Evaluative	Facilitative, Coaching
Frequency	Occasional	Frequent
Formalities	High	Low
Rewards	Individualistic	Grouped, Organisational

Techniques / Methods of Performance Appraisals

Numerous methods have been devised to measure the quantity and quality of performance appraisals. Each of the methods is effective for some purposes for some organisations only. None should be dismissed or accepted as appropriate.

Broadly all methods of appraisals can be divided into two different categories.

- Past Oriented Methods
- Future Oriented Methods

Past Oriented Methods

1. **Rating Scales:** Rating scales consist of several numerical scales representing job related performance criterions such as dependability, initiative, output, attendance, attitude etc. Each scale ranges from excellent to poor. The total numerical scores are computed and the final conclusions are derived. Some of the advantages - adaptability, easy to use, low cost, every type of job can be evaluated, large number of employees covered, no formal training required. Disadvantages - rater's biases.

2. **Checklist:** Under this method, a checklist of statements of traits of employees in the form of Yes or No based questions is prepared. Here the rater only does the reporting or checking and the HR department does the actual evaluation.

Advantages – Economy, ease of administration, limited training required, standardisation. Disadvantages – Rater's biases, use of improper weighs by HR, does not allow rater to give relative ratings.

3. **Forced Choice Method:** The series of statements arranged in the blocks of two or more are given and the rater indicates which statement is true or false. Rater is forced to make a choice. HR department does the actual assessment. Advantages - Absence of personal biases because of forced choice. Disadvantages - Statements may be wrongly framed.

4. **Forced Distribution Method:** Here employees are clustered around a high point on a rating scale. Rater is compelled to distribute the employees on all points on the scale. It is assumed that the performance is conformed to normal distribution.

5. Critical Incidents Method: The approach is focused on certain critical behaviours of the employee that makes all the difference in the performance. Supervisors as and when they occur record such incidents. Advantages - Evaluations are based on actual job behaviours, ratings are supported by descriptions, feedback is easy, reduces biases, chances of subordinate improvement are high. Disadvantages - Negative incidents can be prioritised, forgetting incidents, overly close supervision; feedback may be too much and may appear to be punishment.

6. Behaviourally Anchored Rating Scales: Statements of effective and ineffective behaviours determine the points. They are said to be behaviourally anchored. Rater is supposed to say, which behaviour describes the employee performance. Advantages – helps overcome rating errors. Disadvantages – Suffers from distortions inherent in most rating techniques.

7. Field Review Method: This is an appraisal done by someone outside the employees' own department, usually from corporate or HR department. Advantages - useful for managerial level promotions, when comparable information is needed. Disadvantages - the outsider is generally not familiar with the employees' work environment. Observations of the actual behaviour are not possible.

8. Performance Tests and Observations: This is based on the test of knowledge or skills. The tests may be written or an actual presentation of skills. Tests must be reliable and validated to be useful. Advantage - tests may be apt to measure potential more than actual performance. Disadvantages - tests may suffer if costs of test development or administration are high.

9. Confidential Records: Mostly used by government departments, however its application in industry is not ruled out. Here the report is given in the form of Annual Confidentiality Report (ACR) and may record ratings with respect to the following items; attendance, self expression, team work, leadership, initiative, technical ability, reasoning ability, originality and resourcefulness etc. The system is highly secretive and confidential. Feedback is given only in case of an adverse entry. Disadvantage is that it is highly subjective and ratings can be manipulated because the evaluations are linked to HR actions like promotions etc.

10. Essay Method: In this method the rater writes down the employee description in detail within a number of broad categories like, overall impression of performance, promotion of the employee, existing capabilities and qualifications of performing jobs, strengths and weaknesses and training needs of the employee. Advantage - it is extremely useful in filing information gaps about the employees that often occur in a better-structured checklist. Disadvantages - it is highly dependent upon the writing skills of rater and most of them are not good writers.

11. Cost Accounting Method: Here performance is evaluated from the monetary returns yields to the organisation. Cost to keep employee, and benefit the organisation derives is ascertained. Hence it is more dependent upon cost and benefit analysis.

12. Comparative Evaluation Method (Ranking and Paired Comparisons): These are collection of different methods that compare performance with that of other co-workers. The usual techniques used may be ranking methods and paired comparison method.

- **Ranking Methods:** Superior ranks his worker based on merit, from best to worst. However how best and why best are not elaborated in this method. It is easy to administer and explanation.
- **Paired Comparison Methods:** In this method each employee is rated with another employee in the form of pairs. The number of comparisons may be calculated with the help of a formula as, $N \times (N - 1) / 2$

4.8 Merit Rating

"Merit rating is an assessment according to individual ability which may be rewarded by additional payments to the ordinary rates of pay for the different job".

According to **Yoder,** *"performance appraisal refers to all formal procedures used in working organisations to evaluate personalities and contributions and potential of group members".* Thus merit-rating is a systematic evaluation by the supervisor or some qualified person of an individual worker's performance. The process of merit-rating starts at the time of recruitment and continues throughout the life of an employee in an organisation.

Merit rating is thus the comparative evaluation and analysis of the individual merit of the employees. It is analysis of the individual merit of the employees. It analyses the differences in performance between employees who are working on similar jobs and would therefore earn the same wages. In this task, merit rating accomplishes more than job evaluation. Merit rating is a system of rating employees on the basis of factors such as absenteeism, adaptability, attitude, health, length of service, punctuality and safety record. It is the employee rating achieved through a periodic employee evaluation system, often used as the basis for pay increases and/or promotion.

Definition: Merit rating has been defined as, *the process of evaluating the employees' performance on the job in terms of requirements of the job.*

The characteristics and factors that are considered in merit appraisal of the workers are the following:

1. Co-operation
2. Quality of work done
3. Attendance and regularity
4. Education, skill, experience
5. Character and integrity
6. Initiative

Future Oriented Methods

1. **Management by Objectives:** It means management by objectives and the performance is rated against the achievement of objectives stated by the management. MBO process goes as under.

- Establish goals and desired outcomes for each subordinate
- Setting performance standards
- Comparison of actual goals with goals attained by the employee
- Establish new goals and new strategies for goals not achieved in previous year

Advantage - It is more useful for managerial positions.

Disadvantages - Not applicable to all jobs, allocation of merit pay may result in setting short-term goals rather than important and long-term goals etc.

2. **Psychological Appraisals:** These appraisals are more directed to assess employee's potential for future performance rather than the past one. It is done in the form of in-depth interviews, psychological tests, and discussion with supervisors and review of other evaluations. It is more focused on employees emotional, intellectual, and motivational and other personal characteristics affecting his performance. This approach is slow and costly and may be useful for bright young members who may have considerable potential. However quality of these appraisals largely depends upon the skills of psychologists who perform the evaluation.

3. **Assessment Centers:** This technique was first developed in USA and UK in 1943. An assessment center is a central location where managers may come together to have their participation in job related exercises evaluated by trained observers. It is more focused on observation of behaviours across a series of select exercises or work samples. Assessees are requested to participate in in-basket exercises, work groups, computer simulations, role playing and other similar activities which require same attributes for successful performance in actual job. The characteristics assessed in the assessment center can be assertiveness, persuasive ability, communicating ability, planning and organisational ability, self confidence, resistance to stress, energy level, decision making, sensitivity to feelings, administrative ability, creativity and mental alertness etc. Disadvantages - costs of employees traveling and lodging, psychologists, ratings strongly influenced by assessees inter-personal skills. Solid performers may feel suffocated in simulated situations. Those who are not selected for this also may get affected.

Advantages - A well-conducted assessment center can achieve better forecasts of future performance and progress than other methods of appraisals. Also reliability, content validity and predictive ability are said to be high in assessment centers. The tests also make sure that the wrong people are not hired or promoted. Finally it clearly defines the criteria for selection and promotion.

4. 360-Degree Feedback: It is a technique which is systematic collection of performance data on an individual group, derived from a number of stakeholders like immediate supervisors, team members, customers, peers and self. In fact anyone who has useful information on how an employee does a job may be one of the appraisers. This technique is highly useful in terms of broader perspective, greater self-development and multi-source feedback. 360-degree appraisals are useful to measure inter-personal skills, customer satisfaction and team building skills. However on the negative side, receiving feedback from multiple sources can be intimidating, threatening etc. Multiple raters may be less adept at providing balanced and objective feedback.

4.9 Promotion and Transfer

Promotion

A promotion is the appointment of a member to another position, within the same department or elsewhere in the organisation, involving duties and responsibilities of a more complex or demanding nature and is recognised by a higher pay grade and salary.

A transfer is the appointment of a member to another position within the same department or elsewhere in the organisation, involving duties and responsibilities of a comparable nature and having a similar pay grade and salary. In certain circumstances, the transfer may be at a lesser pay grade or salary.

A promotion is a move up the organisational ladder; job rotation and transfers are lateral moves; demotions are downward moves; and layoffs move employees out. Layoffs, in contrast to dismissals are terminations, sometimes temporary, required for business needs unrelated to worker behaviour or performance. All of these changes bring about shifts in status, and often in pay, of the employees involved.

Seniority vs. Merit in Promotions

Seniority is an employee's length of service in a position, job grouping, or farm operation. An individual who has worked on a farm for three years has more seniority than one who has worked for two. Merit, in contrast, refers to "worth" or "excellence." Merit is more difficult to measure than seniority. In the context of promotion, it relates to relevant qualifications as well as effectiveness of past performance.

Promotion by Seniority

In a straight seniority system where the only factor in allocating jobs is length of service a worker would enter the organisation at the lowest possible level and advance to higher positions as vacancies occur. All prospective farm supervisors and managers would work their way up through the ranks. In a seniority system, length of service is the chief criteria for moving up the ladder.

More typically, seniority counts only within specified job groups. Some groups might contain only one job classification, others several. All managers, for instance, would have once worked as foremen. The benefits and disadvantages of using seniority in promotion decisions are summarised later. The most obvious strength is its undisputed objectivity. Growers may deviate from a system based purely on seniority in order to avoid some of its inherent limitations. Seniority systems tend to reward loyalty and promote cooperation albeit not excellence.

Promotion by Merit

Promotions based on merit advance workers who are best qualified for the position, rather than those with the greatest seniority. When present employees are applying for a position, a worker's past performance is also considered. Effective performance appraisal helps build trust in the system

Merit is not easy to define and measure it often requires difficult subjective evaluations. At some point, someone has to make a judgement about an employee's relative merit. Employees may find it difficult to make a distinction between merits because it is so hard to measure in an objective way and favouritism.

Seniority-based promotions

Advantages

Employees get to experience many jobs on the way up the promotional ladder, provided that they stay long enough and openings develop. Jobs can be grouped into different ladders such that experience on one job constitutes good training for the next. Cooperation between workers is generally not hindered by competition for subjectively determined promotions. Workers need not seek to gain favour with supervisors (through nonproductive means) to obtain advancement. If, for example, a supervisor's direction violates the interests or policy of the ranch, employees would have less fear of reprisal for not following it.

Disadvantages

Some employees may not be able or want to do certain jobs into which a strict seniority system would propel them. (Not all tractor drivers would make good foremen, or would like to be foremen.)

Employees should be able to opt not to accept an opportunity for promotion. Ambitious workers may not be willing to "wait their turn" for higher level jobs that they want. Employee motivation to work as well as possible is not reinforced. Immigrant or ethnic groups new to agriculture, and women, would be underrepresented in higher levels for a long time (since they are the last hired and have least seniority). Employers would tend to hire over skilled people at entry level, so they have the capacity for promotion.

Merit-based promotions
Advantages
Employee job-related abilities can be better matched with jobs to be filled. Motivated and ambitious employees can be rewarded for outstanding performance. Performance is fostered. People can be hired for a specific job, rather than for ability to be promotable.

Disadvantages
Merit and ability are difficult to measure in an objective, impartial way. Supervisors may reward their favourites, rather than the best employees, with high merit ratings. Disruptive conflict may result from worker competition for merit ratings. Unlawful discrimination may enter into merit evaluations.

Seniority vs. Merit in Layoffs
Layoffs are normally considered terminations based on lack of work or capital, rather than on poor employee performance. Layoffs are often temporary. They occur with the expectation that workers will be hired back if and when they are needed. When all workers are laid-off at the same time, there is little need to discuss seniority and merit considerations. But when partial or gradual layoffs take place, difficult decisions have to be made.

Layoffs of year-round employees may require a different approach than that of seasonal workers. Decisions involving the layoff of non-seasonal personnel may well be the hardest or most heart wrenching labour management decision you have to make. The expectation with year-round employment is that workers will hold on to their positions as long as they do a good job and the enterprise is economically viable. Certainly, in considering such a mix, greater weight is probably given to seniority considerations in layoff than in promotion decisions.

Arguments that favour making layoffs in reverse order of seniority, that is, the last hired, the first to go include:

(1) The longer employees have worked for an enterprise, the more loyalty they are due. Other employees will observe and be affected by how senior employees are treated.

(2) Senior employees who lose their jobs may have greater difficulty finding another job at the equivalent pay and benefit level than younger workers.

(3) Layoffs by merit may lead to age discrimination law suits if older workers are disproportionately terminated.

The principal argument favouring merit to determine layoff decisions is:

(1) Management should retain the best people to do the job, especially when functioning with fewer employees.

Employers sometimes offer special retirement packages (VRS) to entice more senior personnel to retire. This is often done in an effort to save money in situations where senior personnel earn disproportionately higher wages.

Open or Close System

Promotion policies may affect employees' hopes for advancement and the productivity of the workforce. Often employers feel compelled to promote from within their workforce, fearing the loss of the loyalty and enthusiasm of present employees. Promotion from within encourages employees to view the organisation as one offering them career growth. Unfortunately, a tradition of promoting from within may also mean forgoing the most vital management prerogative: filling positions with well-qualified personnel. It is a mistake to assume that superior performance in one job will always translate into equivalent success after promotion to a new position. Personnel who move from technical jobs to supervisory ones, or from "doing" jobs to managing ones, may not always be skilled in handling the added responsibility and power. Occasionally, you may have to consider the demotion of a worker who has not succeeded after being promoted.

Alternatives to Promotions

At times employees may want job growth when no promotions are available. Workers sometimes fall into the trap of thinking the only evidence of career success is a promotion. Likewise, some employers feel the only way to reward good workers is to promote them. Personnel who want a promotion will sometimes demand a change or threaten to leave for a different job. In such cases, if a promotion is not possible, employers may encourage the worker in a positive way to pursue other career possibilities with reactions such as, "Here, we don't try to keep people back," "When the need arises, we help our workers find another job," and even, "We feel we are a stepping stone to other jobs. We are pretty proud of the places our employees have gone to after working for us." At times such attitudes are the only practical solution. But, as we see below there are plenty of circumstances where qualified employees can grow within their present position.

In considering the best strategy to use, you may ask:

(1) Does the employee want to advance?
(2) Does he want more responsibility or more variety?

In the latter case, the worker can be given different duties or assignments that constitute a transfer rather than a promotion.

Transfer

Lateral Transfer: A lateral transfer is a move to a position with the same or similar job title in the same pay grade. Such transfers provide opportunities to work with new colleagues, to master a different range of skills, or transfer special skills and experience to a new environment.

Transfers and job rotation are forms of enlargement entailing movement from one job to another of comparable responsibility. Transfers usually last for a longer term while job rotation may imply several short term job changes. In addition, some rotations are cyclical and involve going through the same set of jobs over and over. In a bank, for instance, workers may be part of a job rotation cycle from being cashier to distributing loans. Besides alleviating possible boredom, transfers and job rotations expose workers to more tasks. When an absence or turnover occurs, it helps to have other knowledgeable employees who can perform the vacated job. Morale can suffer when transfers require employees to relocate. A raise in pay may help assignments carry unique challenges and opportunities

Transfers Resulting from Reassignment

When there is a significant business need, division/department heads have the authority to transfer employees from one position to another at the same grade and salary in the same division/department without announcing the vacancy through the posting process. In such cases, the division/department head should discuss the situation and submit a memorandum to the Employment section of the Human Resources Department in advance of the reassignment, indicating the rationale for the change and, if applicable, attaching a Personnel Action Form (PAF) for the employee. In effecting such transfers, the department should attempt to make the most effective use of the employee's skills and abilities and should consider the employee's interest whenever possible.

Distinction between Transfer and Promotion

Promotion takes place when an employee moves to a position higher than the one formerly occupied. Transfer is the movement of an employee from one job to another without involving any change in his status, duties and responsibilities and compensation. The distinction between promotion and transfer can be drawn on the following grounds:

(a) **Nature:** In case of promotion, new position carries higher pay, status and job conditions and compared with the old while in case of transfer, pay, status, responsibilities and job conditions are almost the same.

(b) **Objects:** Promotion aims at recruiting the right man on the job from the lower rank within the organisation while transfer aims at maintaining equilibrium between demand and supply of the employees by shifting the employees from one job to another or from one department to another.

(c) **Policy:** Promotion as a part of personnel programmes, helps the employees to increase their efficiency but transfer is used as a technique in training programmes.

4.10 Job Description

Job analysis is important from the view point of manpower planning, recruitment, selection and placement, induction of new trainees, promotion and transfer, training and development, job evaluation, performance appraisal, etc. It shows that the study of job analysis occupies an important place in the study of Human Resource Management. In job analysis, as a process, by collecting necessary information, study is done relating to operations and responsibilities of a specific job. Dale Yoder describes job analysis as *"the procedure by which the facts with respect to each job are systematically discovered and noted"*. Job descriptions, job specification, job evaluation, etc., are important job analysis components.

4.10.1 Meaning and Definitions of Job Description

Job description is one of the broad areas of job analysis while the other is job specification. Job specification gives details relating to the candidate who is supposed to perform duties on the job, such as qualifications, experience, abilities, skills etc. While job description gives details of the job in respect of duties, responsibilities, etc. Job description is a brief and compact written statement of duties, responsibilities and it is based on job analysis which gathers, assembles and analyses the factual information about a specific job. In other words, job description is a systematic, summarised record about the specific job. Such description gives an indication about the physical, mental and other general requirements required for performing the job. It also makes clear what is to be done, how it is to be done and why it is to be done. Its basic objective is to differentiate it from other jobs and to set its outer limits. Job description helps the management to establish assessment standards and objectives.

According to **Edwin B. Flippo**, *"The first and immediate product of job analysis is the job description. As its title indicates, this document is basically descriptive in nature and constitutes a record of existing and pertinent job facts"*.

While **Maurice W. Cuming** makes it clear that, *"Job description is a broad statement of the purpose, scope, duties and responsibilities of a particular job"*.

From the above stated definitions and discussion done, we can define job description as the organised, factual and written statement specifying the duties, responsibilities, requirements of a particular or a specific job prepared on the basis of job analysis.

4.10.2 Contents or Components of Job Description

A job description usually contains the following information:

(a) Job Identification

This includes the job title, alternative title, department and division, plant and code number of the job. The job title helps to identify the job and department and division indicate the name of the department, its place, whether maintenance, mechanical or any other department.

(b) Job Summary

It is a brief write-up what the job is all about. In fact, it is a quick capsule explanation of the job in one or two sentences.

(c) Job Duties and Responsibilities

This portion of the job description gives a comprehensive list of duties to be performed. It is regarded as the heart of the job description. Job duties also make clear the job activities. Responsibilities related to the custody of cash, supervision, training to subordinates are also described in this part.

(d) Relation to Other Jobs

This section makes clear the vertical relationship of work flow and procedures and also the location of the job in the organisation by indicating the job immediately below or above it in the job hierarchy.

(e) Supervision

This section is related to supervision making clear the number of employees to be supervised along with their job titles, the extent and degree of supervision involved i.e., general, intermediate or close supervision.

(f) Information about Machines, Tools and Equipments, Materials

In this part, information relating to major type or trade name of the machines, tools, equipments and raw materials used is given.

(g) Working Conditions

It specifies the conditions under which the employees have to work i.e. heat, cold, dust, moisture, fumes, etc. Because of this, job holders get an idea about the environment in which they have to work.

(h) Hazards

Many jobs are hazardous involving the risks of accidents. Hazardous conditions are particularly noted making clear the nature of risks of life, limbs as well as the possibilities of their occurrence.

From the above discussion, we come to know about the contents of a job description. But to remember them easily, the points to be considered relating to the job are enlisted below:

1. Title of the Job.
2. Alternative title, if any.
3. Organisational location of the job.
4. Designation of an immediate supervisor and a subordinate, and supervision given and received.
5. Definitions of job purposes and job duties.
6. Definitions of unusual terms, if any.
7. Extent and limits of authority.
8. Relation to other jobs.
9. Additional responsibility requirements.

10. Materials tools and equipments etc., required as per nature of the job.
11. Complete list of duties to be performed according to daily, hourly, weekly, monthly, etc., estimated time to be spent on each duty.
12. Working conditions i.e. location, time, accuracy, various types of hazards, etc.
13. Salary levels i.e., pay, D.A. and other allowances, bonus, methods of payment, etc.
14. Training and developmental facilities.
15. Promotional chances and channels.

4.10.3 Process of Writing a Job Description

A job analyst writes the job description and for that purpose, he consults the workers concerned or both, workers and supervisors. First, preliminary draft is prepared, then it is shown to the employees concerned and after their comments, suggestions, the final draft is prepared. For writing the job description any one or a combination of two or more methods mentioned as follows can be used:

(a) For the purpose of required information, a suitable questionnaire is asked to be filled in by the immediate supervisor.

(b) Job analyst may gather necessary information pertaining to the job from the worker, and

(c) Job analyst observes the actual work when the processes done by the worker and on that basis, he completes the job description.

It should be noted that job descriptions are not perfect reflections of the jobs; they are based on certain variables. Even when, the final draft of job description is prepared, it should be reviewed systematically. A job tends to be dynamic and hence a job description can quickly go out of date. Job descriptions are therefore required to be constantly revised and kept up-to-date.

4.10.4 Guidelines for Writing a Job Description

As already made clear, a job description is an important document which provides organisational information i.e., location in structure, authority, etc., and functional information i.e., what activities pertain to the specific job. From the job description, one comes to know the scope of job activities, major responsibilities, positioning of the job in the organisation. A job description makes clear what the worker must do to meet the demands of the job. It is the description of the job and not of the job holders.

According to some experts, the job descriptions must be written in detail and in terms of work flow. While others feel that the job descriptions should be written in terms of goals or results to be achieved. There is always a view that duties and responsibilities must also be included in the job descriptions. Thus, how to write the job description seems to be a subjective issue depending upon the needs of the organisation. But to study the topic 'Job Description', let us consider its following two aspects:

[A] Important guidelines for writing a job description or characteristics of a good job description, and

[B] How to write a job description.

[A] Important Guidelines for Writing Job Description

There is no particular format of writing a job description. Some experts like Dale have developed certain guidelines for writing a job description.

Important guidelines are given below:

(1) The job description should make clear the nature, scope etc., of the job including all important relationships.

(2) It should be brief, factual and precise. Moreover, active verbs should be used to give a clear picture of the job avoiding opinions.

(3) There should be a proper job title suggesting the nature of job.

(4) In the job description, primary, secondary and other related duties and responsibilities should be clearly defined and explained.

(5) It should include a comprehensive job summary. Specific words should be used to show kinds of work, degree of complexity, degree of skills, abilities required, various possible problems, hazards, degree and type of accountability, etc.

(6) Job description should be easily understandable and there should not be any sort of ambiguity.

(7) Job requirements should be clearly stated in the job description.

(8) The extent of supervision should be clearly stated.

(9) The reporting relationship should be clearly indicated.

(10) It should make clear the opportunities for career development.

(11) Utility of the job description in meeting the basic requirements should be examined from the extent of understanding the job by reading the job description by the new employees.

(12) There can be changes in the nature of the job. Considering the changes, the job description should be modified and made up-to-date from time to time.

[B] How to Write a Job Description

Valerie, Grant and British Institute of Management have stated in "Personnel Administration and Industrial Relations" and "Job Evaluation: A Practical Guide for Managers – 1970" respectively, point-wise fairly typical pattern of writing the job description generally used by many companies. Accordingly, following are the points which are considered while writing the job description:

(1) Each major task or responsibility pertaining to the job is stated in a separate paragraph.

(2) The paragraphs are numbered properly and arranged in a logical order, task sequence or importance.

(3) Sentences begin with an active verb such as 'types letters', 'interviews the candidates', "collects, sort out routes and distributes the mails", etc.

(4) Accuracy and simplicity are emphasised rather than an elegant style.

(5) Brevity is usually considered as an important aspect but it is largely conditioned by the type of job being analysed and the need for accuracy.

(6) Examples of work performed are quoted in order to make the job description explicit.

(7) Job descriptions, particularly when they are used as the bases for training, often incorporate details of which may be encountered in operator tasks and safety check-points.

(8) Statements of opinion such as "dangerous situations are encountered" are avoided.

(9) When job descriptions are written for supervisory jobs, the main factors such as manning, cost control, etc., are identified and listed. Each factor is then broken down into a series of elements with a note on the supervisor's responsibility.

In the British Institute of Management's Publication "Job Evaluation: A Practical Guide for Managers (1970)", the following four guidelines of writing a job description are given:

(a) Give a clear, concise and readily understandable picture of the whole job;

(b) Describe in sufficient detail each of the main duties and responsibilities;

(c) Indicate the extent of direction received and supervision given, and

(d) Ensure that a new employee understands the job if he reads the job description.

No doubt, there are many difficulties in writing a job description. It may not be hundred per cent correct. But it is certain that it is useful method of providing necessary information for making decisions in personnel activities. It is a used for job evaluation, providing safety measures, employee evaluation, improvements in the job, etc.

4.11 Job Evaluation

Job evaluation is a systematic and orderly process of determining the worth of a job in relation to other jobs. In job evaluation, a systematic comparison is done in order to determine the worth of one job relative to another. The basis of a sound wage structure is job evaluation. The important methods of job evaluation are: (1) Ranking, (2) Classification, (3) Factor comparison, (4) Point method and (5) Market pricing method. The important objectives of job evaluation are mentioned below:

(a) To provide a standard procedure for determining the relative worth or value of each job in a plant.
(b) To make sure that like wages are paid to all qualified employees on like work and to avoid discrimination.
(c) To make available a factual basis for fixing wage rates for similar jobs within the industry.
(d) To maintain accurate, complete descriptions of each distinct job in the entire plant.
(e) To provide fair and accurate consideration of all employees for advancement, transfer etc.
(f) To provide necessary information on the work organisation for selection, recruitment, training etc. This helps the employees and their organisation to take necessary decisions.

Job evaluation is defined as a practical technique, designed to enable trained and experienced staff to judge the size/worth of one job relative to others. It does not directly determine pay levels, but will establish the basis for an internal ranking of jobs. It is essentially a comparative process. Evaluation is done by assessing the job pressure. Factors that contribute to this job pressure, e.g. physical strength required, knowledge required, are assessed and the result is a numerical estimate of the total job pressure. Job evaluation is concerned with jobs, not people. It is not the person that is being evaluated. All jobs in an organisation will be evaluated using an agreed job evaluations scheme. Job evaluators will need to gain a thorough understanding of the job. The job is assessed as if it were being carried out in a fully competent and acceptable manner. Job evaluation is based on judgement and is not scientific. The real test of the evaluation results is their acceptability to all participants. Job evaluation can aid organisational problem solving as it highlights duplication of tasks and gaps between jobs and functions.

Job Evaluation Process include:
- Establish job evaluation objectives
- Conduct job analysis – results in job description and job specification
- Job evaluation programme
- Wage Survey
- Employee classification

Job Evaluation – Methods
1. **Analytical methods**
   (a) **Point Ranking Method**
   - In this method the number of grades is first decided.
   - Select key jobs. Identify the factors common to all the identified jobs such as skill, effort, responsibility, working conditions etc.

- Fix a relative value for each key factor.
- Divide each major factor into a number of sub factors. Each sub factor is defined and expressed clearly in the order of importance, preferably along a scale.
- Construct degrees for each sub factors.
- Assign points to each degree.
- A given job is placed in a particular grade depending on the number of points it scores.

(b) Factor Comparison Method
- Begins with the selection of factors which include mental requirements, skill requirements, physical exertion, responsibility and job condition.
- The factors are assumed constant for all the jobs.
- Assign money value/ weight age to each factor depending upon the nature of the job.
- Each factor is ranked individually for each job.
- The worth of the job is obtained by adding together all the points.

2. Non-Analytical Methods
(a) Ranking Method
- In this method the evaluation committee assesses the worth of each job on the basis of its title or on its contents.
- Each job is compared with others and its place is determined.
- Normally Jobs are arranged according to the difficulty in performing them.

(b) Job-grading Method / Classification Method
- In this method the number of grades is first decided upon, and the factors corresponding to these grades are then determined.
- Facts about jobs are collected and are matched with the grades and jobs are assigned to each grade.
- The essential requirement of job grading method is to frame grade descriptions to cover differences in degree of skill, responsibility, and other job characteristics.

Job-grading Method / Classification Method

Brief description of job classification in an office is mentioned below:

1. **Class I** - Executives: Further classification under this category may be Office manager, Deputy office manager, Office Superintendent, Departmental supervisor, etc.
2. **Class II** - Skilled workers: Under this category may come the Purchase assistant, Cashier, Receipts clerk, etc.
3. **Class III** - Semiskilled workers: Under this category may come Steno typists, Machine-operators, Switchboard operators, etc.
4. **Class IV** - Semiskilled workers: This category comprises File clerks, office boys etc.

4.12 Job Enlargement

Job Enlargement, is *a job design technique in which the number of tasks associated with a job is increased (and appropriate training provided) to add greater variety to activities, thus reducing monotony.*

Job enlargement is considered a horizontal restructuring method in that the job is enlarged by adding related tasks. Job enlargement may also result in greater workforce flexibility.

Job enlargement is another method of job design when any organisation wishes to adopt proper job design it can opt for job enlargement. Job enlargement involves combining various activities at the same level in the organisation and adding them to the existing job. It increases the scope of the job. It is also called the horizontal expansion of job activities.

Definition: *Job Enlargement is the horizontal expansion of a job.* It involves the addition of tasks at the same level of skill and responsibility. It is done to keep workers from getting bored. It is different than job enrichment.

Examples: Small companies may not have as many opportunities for promotions, so they try to motivate employees through job enlargement.

Job enlargement can be explained with the help of the following example - If Mr. A is working as an executive with a company and is currently performing 3 activities on his job after job enlargement or through job enlargement we add 4 more activities to the existing job so now Mr. A performs 7 activities on the job.

It must be noted that the new activities which have been added should belong to the same hierarchy level in the organisation. By job enlargement we provide a greater variety of activities to the individual so that we are in a position to increase the interest of the job and make maximum use of employee's skill. Job enlargement is also essential when policies like VRS are implemented in the company.

Job enlargement is doing different tasks and not just the same thing all the time. It may involve taking on more duties and adds variety to a person's job. Horizontal loading is often used which is giving people more jobs to do that require the same level of skill.

Job enlargement contradicts the principles of specialisation and the division of labour whereby work is divided into small units, each of which is performed repetitively by an individual worker. Some motivational theories suggest that the boredom and alienation caused by the division of labour can actually cause efficiency to fall. Thus, job enlargement seeks to motivate workers through reversing the process of specialisation. A typical approach might be to replace assembly lines with modular work; instead of an employee repeating the same step on each product, they perform several tasks on a single item. In order for employees to be provided with Job Enlargement they will need to be retrained in new fields which can prove to be a lengthy process. However results have shown that this process can see its effects weaken after a period of time, as even the enlarged job role becomes mundane, this in turn can lead to similar levels of demotivation and job dissatisfaction at the expense of increased training levels and costs. The continual enlargement of a job over time is also known as 'job creep,' which can lead to an unmanageable workload.

Advantages of Job Enlargement

- **Variety of skills:** Job enlargement helps the organisation to improve and increase the skills of the employee due to organisation as well as the individual benefit.
- **Improves earning capacity:** Due to job enlargement the person learns many new activities. When such people apply for jobs to other companies they can bargain for more salary.
- **Wide range of activities:** Job enlargement provides wide range of activities for employees. Since a single employee handles multiple activities the company can try and reduce the number of employee's. This reduces the salary bill for the company.

Disadvantages of Job Enlargement

- **Increases work burden:** Job enlargement increases the work of the employee and not every company provides incentives and extra salary for extra work. Therefore the efforts of the individual may remain unrecognised.
- **Increasing frustration of the employee:** In many cases employees end up being frustrated because increased activities do not result in increased salaries.
- **Problem with union members:** Many union members may misunderstand job enlargement as exploitation of worker and may take objection to it.

4.13 Job Enrichment

Job enrichment means a vertical expansion of a job. It is different from job enlargement which means the horizontal expansion of a job.

Job enrichment makes the job more meaningful, enjoyable and satisfying. It gives the workers more autonomy for planning and controlling the job. It also gives the workers more responsibility. Job enrichment gives the workers opportunities for achievement, recognition, advancement and growth. So, the workers are motivated to work harder. Therefore, Job enrichment makes the job a source of motivation.

Features of Job Enrichment

The characteristics or features of job enrichment are:

- **Nature of Job:** Job enrichment is a vertical expansion of the job. The workers are given jobs, which require higher-level knowledge, skills and responsibilities. Job enrichment improves the quality of the job.

- **Objective:** The objective of job enrichment is to make the job more lively and challenging. So, the job is a source of motivation for the workers.
- **Positive Results:** Job enrichment gives positive results if the workers are highly skilled. This is because workers are given opportunities to show initiative and innovation while doing their job.
- **Direction and Control:** Job enrichment encourages self-discipline. It does not believe in external direction and control.

Fig 4.2: Job Enrichment

Advantages of Job Enrichment

The importance or merits or advantages of job enrichment are:

- Job enrichment is useful to both the workers and the organisation.
- The worker gets achievement, recognition and self-actualisation.
- The worker gets a sense of belonging to the organisation.
- The worker finds the job meaningful.
- Job enrichment reduces absenteeism, labour-turnover and grievances.
- It motivates the workers to give best performance.

Limitations of Job Enrichment

The shortcomings or demerits or limitations of job enrichment are:

- In many cases, job enrichment does not give the expected results.

- It makes many changes in the job. So many workers oppose it.
- It has limited use for highly skilled managers and professionals. This is because their jobs are already challenging.
- The consent of workers is not taken before implementing job enrichment.
- Managers force the workers to accept job enrichment, which is not good.

Difference between Job Enlargement and Job Enrichment

The difference between job enrichment and job enlargement is quality and quantity. Job enrichment means improvement, or an increase with the help of upgrading and development, whereas job enlargement means to add more duties, and an increased workload. By job enrichment, an employee finds satisfaction in respect to their position and personal growth potential, whereas job enlargement refers to having additional duties and responsibilities in a current job description.

Job enlargement is a vehicle employers use to put additional workload on employees, perhaps in economical downtime. Due to downsizing, an employee might feel lucky to have a job at all, despite the fact that his duties and responsibilities have increased. Another approach is that by adding more variety and enlarging the responsibilities will provide the chance of enhancement and more productivity. Job enrichment involves organising and planning in order to gain more control over their duties and work as a manager. The execution of plans and evaluation of results motivates workers and relieves boredom. Job enlargement and job enrichment are both useful for motivating workers to perform their tasks enthusiastically.

Although job enlargement and enrichment have a relationship with each other, they also possess some distinct features that differentiate them, such as area of expansion, mutual reliance, allocation of duties and responsibilities, motivation and profundity. Job enrichment is largely dependent on job enlargement, whereas job enlargement has no such dependency. Job enlargement expands horizontally when compared to job enrichment, which expands vertically. Vertical growth of job or augmentation is helpful to obtain managerial rights.

In spite of mutual dependency, managerial duties are sanctioned, as in the case of enhancement. The employee focuses more on job depth, which does not happen in job enlargement. Job enrichment has a greater motivational impact than job enlargement.

The job enlargement theory involving horizontal expansion to increase job satisfaction and productivity is relatively simple, and applied in numerous situations. Job enrichment, when compared to job enlargement, not only includes more duties and responsibilities, but also gives the right of decision making and control.

4.14 Job Rotation

Job Rotation is a management approach where employees are shifted between two or more assignments or jobs at regular intervals of time in order to expose them to all verticals of an organisation. It is a pre-planned approach with an objective to test the employee skills and competencies in order to place him or her at the right place. In addition to it, it reduces the monotony of the job and gives them a wider experience and helps them gain more insights.

Job rotation is a well-planned practice to reduce the boredom of doing same type of job everyday and explore the hidden potential of an employee. The process serves the purpose of both the management and the employees. It helps management in discovering the talent of employees and determining what he or she is best at. On the other hand, it gives an individual a chance to explore his or her own interests and gain experience in different fields or operations.

Job Rotation Objectives

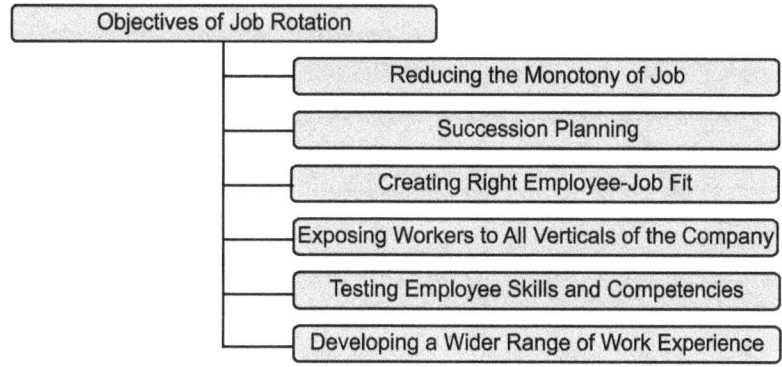

Fig 4.3: Objectives of Job Rotation

- **Reducing Monotony of the Job:** The first and foremost objective of job rotation is to reduce the monotony and repetitiveness involved in a job. It allows employees to experience different type of jobs and motivates them to perform well at each stage of job replacement.
- **Succession Planning:** The concept of succession planning is 'Who will replace whom'. Its main function in job rotation is to develop a pool of employees who can be placed at a senior level when someone gets retired or leaves the organisation. The idea is to create an immediate replacement of a high-worth employee from within the organisation.

- **Creating Right-Employee Job Fit:** The success of an organisation depends on the on-job productivity of its employees. If they're rightly placed, they will be able to give the maximum output. In case, they are not assigned the job that they are good at, it creates a real big problem for both employee as well as organisation. Therefore, fitting a right person in right vacancy is one of the main objectives of job rotation.
- **Exposing Workers to All Verticals of the Company:** Another main function of the job rotation process is to expose workers to all verticals or operations of the organisation in order to make them aware how company operates and how tasks are performed. It gives them a chance to understand the working of the organisation and different issues that crop up while working.
- **Testing Employee Skills and Competencies:** Testing and analysing employee skills and competencies and then assigning them the work that they excel at is one of the major functions of the job rotation process. It is done by moving them to different jobs and assignments and determining their proficiency and aptitude. Placing them what they are best at increases their on-job productivity.
- **Developing a Wider Range of Work Experience:** Employees, usually don't want to change their area of operations. Once they start performing a specific task, they don't want to shift from their comfort zone. Through job rotation, managers prepare them in advance to have a wider range of work experience and develop different skills and competencies. It is necessary for overall development of an individual. Along with this, they understand the problems of various departments and try to adjust or adapt accordingly.

Job rotation is a well planned management approach that is beneficial both for employees and management.

Points to Remember

- **Training** is a planned, organised and controlled activity designed to express some aspect or aspects of present job performance. Training is skill oriented and it is usually intended for the short run welfare of the economy (i.e. organisation). Training is also a key ingredient in the motivation of individuals. An untrained, unskilled employee feels very insecure, lacking the self-condifence necessary for comfortable group relations
- **Training is given to the employees in order:**
    (i) to enhance the existing knowledge, skills and abilities, performance capabilities of the employees and to acquire new skills, abilities, knowledge for improving their qualities.
    (ii) to increase efficiency and productivity of the employees.

(iii) to help an organisation to fulfil its future personnel needs.
(iv) to improve health and safety of employees.
(v) to prevent wastages, wear and tear, obsolescence etc.
(vi) to improve organisational climate.
(vii) to help employees achieve personal growth and development.
(viii) to improve morale of employees.
(ix) to keep abreast of (i.e. up to date with) developments in technical and management fields and also to inculcate a sense of appreciation for other functional areas and an understanding of the linkage of their activities with other areas.
(x) to induct new employees into the organisation.

- **Types of training programmes:** 1. Induction Training, 2. Job training, 3. Training for promotions, 4.Supervisory training, 5. Management development training.
- **Classification of Training methods:**

    (a) Knowledge-based methods,

    (b) On the job oriented training methods,

    (c) Simulation methods,

    (d) Experimental methods.

- **Types of Training methods**

    Types of training include: 1. Lectures, 2. Programmed instruction method, 3. Conference method, 4. Case method, 5. Role – play, 6. T-group training method, 7. Job instruction training, 8. Coaching, 9. Vestibule training, 10. Job rotation, 11. Business or management games, 12. In basket exercise method, 13. Behavioural modelling, 14. Brainstorming sessions, 15. Multiple management method, 16. Incident method, 17. Managerial grid, 18. Committee Assignment method.

- **Systems Approach to Training (SAT)** is a practical, results-oriented training program that provides people with the skills and the knowledge to do their tasks correctly, efficiently, and with confidence.
- **Performance Appraisal** is the assessment of individual's performance in a systematic way. It is a developmental tool used for all round development of the employee and the organisation.

    Merit rating is an assessment according to individual ability which may be rewarded by additional payments to the ordinary rates of pay for the different job.

- A **promotion** is the appointment of a member to another position, within the same department or elsewhere in the organisation, involving duties and responsibilities of a more complex or demanding nature and is recognised by a higher pay grade and salary.

- A **transfer** is the appointment of a member to another position within the same department or elsewhere in the organisation, involving duties and responsibilities of a comparable nature and having a similar pay grade and salary. In certain circumstances, the transfer may be at a lesser pay grade or salary.
- **Job description** is a broad statement of the purpose, scope, duties and responsibilities of a particular job. Job description is a brief and compact written statement of duties, responsibilities and it is based on job analysis which gathers, assembles and analyses the factual information about a specific job. In other words, job description is a systematic, summarised record about the specific job. Such description gives an indication about the physical, mental and other general requirements required for performing the job.
- **Components of Job Description**: 1. Job Identification, 2. Job Summary, 3. Job Duties and Responsibilities, 4. Relation to other jobs, 5. Supervision, 6. Information about machines, tools and equipments, materials, 7. Working conditions, 8. Hazards
- **Job evaluation** is a systematic and orderly process of determining the worth of a job in relation to other jobs.
- **Job enrichment** means a vertical expansion of a job. It is different from job enlargement. Job enlargement means a horizontal expansion of a job.
- **Job Rotation** is a management approach where employees are shifted between two or more assignments or jobs at regular intervals of time in order to expose them to all verticals of an organisation. It is a pre-planned approach with an objective to test the employee skills and competencies in order to place him or her at the right place. In addition to it, it reduces the monotony of the job and gives them a wider experience and helps them gain more insights.

Questions for Discussion

1. Define and explain the term ' Training'. State its objectives.
2. Explain the different Types of Training or what are the various methods of training?
3. Explain the 'Evaluation of Training '.
4. Explain the importance of performance appraisal.
5. Define merit rating.
6. What are the objectives of training evaluation? Explain any one model of training evaluation.
7. Explain in detail various 'Rating Errors" in performance appraisal process.
8. Explain the concept of merit rating and its methods.

9. Discuss concepts of job enlargement and job enrichment. How is job enlargement different from job enrichment?
10. Write short notes on:
    (a) Job Description
    (b) Job Evaluation
    (c) Job Rotation
    (d) Training Need Evaluation
    (e) Training Calendar

Questions from Previous Pune University Examinations

1. Discuss the concept of Job Enlargement and Job Enrichment. How is Job Enlargement different from Job Enrichment? **(April - 2012)**
2. What is Merit Rating? Discuss its importance in the organisation with various methods of merit Rating. **(April - 2012)**
3. Write short notes: **(April - 2012)**
    (a) Job Rotation
    (b) Training Calendar
4. Explain in detail various methods of Performance Appraisal. **(Oct. - 2012)**
5. What is Training? Explain the difference between Training, Development and Education. **(Oct. - 2012)**
6. Write short notes: **(Oct. - 2012)**
    (a) Job Description
    (b) Merit Rating - Need and Importance
7. Explain what is Training? Explain various methods of Training in detail. **(April - 2013)**
8. Write short notes: **(April - 2013)**
    (a) Job Enrichment
    (b) Promotion

Chapter 5...

Recent Trends and Problems in Motivation, Retention, Attrition, Downsizing and Outsourced Manpower

Contents ...

Introduction

    5.1 Recent Trends and Problems in Motivation

    5.2 Recent Trends and Problems in Retention

    5.3 Recent Trends and Problems in Attrition

    5.4 Downsizing

    5.5 Manpower Outsourcing

    5.6 International Human Resource Management (IHRM)

    5.7 Multiculturism/Multiculturalism

    5.8 Cross Cultural Training (CCT)

    5.9 New Terms

- Points to Remember
- Case Study
- Questions for Discussion
- Questions from Previous Pune University Examinations

Learning Objectives ...

- To be aware of the recent trends and problems in the areas of motivation, retention, attrition
- To learn about downsizing and outsourced manpower
- To gain knowledge of the concept of International Human Resource Management
- To be able to discuss the concepts of multiculturalism and cross cultural training

Introduction

Human resource management (HRM) has always been a very challenging aspect of any business. Especially with so much happening in the world of Human Resource, change, indeed is the constant when we talk about Human Resource Management.

There are new trends in the world of HR emerging every now and then and it is extremely important for anybody associated with the world of business to know about such contemporary emerging issues. In this era of globalisation human resource has walked into a zone of new technology and certain emerging issues of management. Here, we would discuss about the most relevant emerging and contemporary issues about human resource.

The issues that have very clearly emerged in recent times are planning, acquisition and development which include motivation, retention, attrition, downsizing and outsourcing of manpower.

The innovation of HRM happens to be the most striking part of the latest emerging issues in the world of human resources. Crafting of new business strategies in the light of human resource is a major emergence in this particular field. Organisational restructuring is just another important and notable aspect of emerging human resource management issues. Creation of social networking in support of business is a notable aspect of the new trends. Enabling companies to be global, leading to superior performance and creating knowledge workforce are other notable parts of these emerging issues.

5.1 Recent Trends and Problems in Motivation

Motivation is the set of forces that cause people to behave in certain ways. Motivation is a human psychological characteristic that contributes to a person's degree of commitment. Motivating is the management process of influencing people's behaviour based on the knowledge of 'what makes people tick'.

Motivation is derived from the word motive. *"A motive is an inner state that energises, activates or moves and directs or channels behaviour towards goals".*

Motivation is a process that starts with a physiological or psychological deficiency or need that activates behaviour or a drive that is aimed at a goal or incentive.

Motivation of employees in HRM is about measures aimed at encouraging staff in order to enhance their productivity. Motivation is essential, since it ensures quality work and better output from employees. Motivation can be achieved through financial and psychological rewards as well as good working conditions.

Motivation is important in getting and retaining people. Motivation tools act as the glue that links individuals to organisational goals, in addition, make individuals go beyond the job and be creative.

Types of Motives

Motives are divided into categories Primary motives, General motives and Secondary motives.

Primary Motives: These motives are unlearned and physiologically based. They include hunger, sleep, avoidance of pain, and maternal concern.

General Motives: These motives are unlearned but not physiological based. These motives include curiosity, manipulation and activity motives and the affection motive.

Secondary Motives: Secondary motives are closely tied to the learning concept. A motive must be learned in order to be included in the secondary classification. Important among them are achievement, affiliation power, security, status and immediate feedback.

Steps in Motivation

According to Jucius, the following are the steps that should be adopted in motivation:
1. Sizing up situations requiring motivation.
2. Preparing a set of motivating tools.
3. Selecting and applying an appropriate motivator.
4. Following up the results of the application.

Current Trends in Motivation

Today's workforce is diverse. Full time employee needs, part time employee needs and retired and rejoined employee needs are different. The needs of female employees will be different than that of male employees.

Today is an extremely dynamic and volatile work environment marked by continued turbulence in the economy. Managers face a difficult challenge of motivating and retaining employees in an environment of increased uncertainties.

These different types of needs of different types of employees influence the behavioural pattern of each type and give scope for the formulation of different types of motivational factors. Flexibility is one important factor which motivates and satisfies the needs of employees. Solutions such as flexibility in time, flexibility in operations etc. have emerged today to motivate workers.

"Virtual office", the modern concept provides opportunity to employees to work from home. Of course technology has to be adapted for this purpose. Besides flexi time operations and compressed work weeks, job sharing, telecommunicating, pay for performance, employee stock options, motivating minimum wage employees, matching people to jobs, adaptation of equity concepts are some of the current issues of motivating the work force in an organisation. These issues are considered as motivating tools and are implemented according to the situations that prevail in the organisation.

Another trend is the importance given to the quality of jobs being offered. Many sources indicate that certain jobs and goal setting can enhance performance. One such factor can be termed as job design. A well defined job design would enhance motivation, satisfaction and performance of the employee. A job design has various dimensions such as job enrichment, job engineering and quality of work life.

Nowadays rewards, recognition, stability, cultural background has become very important in the organisational environment and this can be attributed due to several reasons. Employees worldwide are asked to do more and the organisations want this to be done autonomously. This can only happen if the employee is induced to work by providing him various benefits which are otherwise not part of their pay cheque.

Problems in Motivation

Motivational problems can lead to performance issues that cost an organisation lakhs of rupees in losses each year. A lack of motivation can lead to delays in the employee's completion of work and simple but expensive mistakes. Unfortunately, several issues may weaken an employee's motivation and leave him unproductive.

Low Self-Confidence

Confidence enhances an employee's motivation; he believes that he can perform the tasks necessary to achieve his goals. Confidence contributes to his willingness to persevere and complete tasks. If the employee lacks confidence, he feels unworthy and is unable to make decisions or remain motivated until an objective is accomplished. Lacking self-confidence, the employee is unable to form good work relationships or assert himself, both of which are important if the employee is to be successful in the workplace. In addition, the employee will procrastinate or apply limited effort to ensure that these issues, and not himself, are the reasons the employee fails.

Low Expectations for Success

Positive expectations of success enhance an employee's motivation. If an employer has high expectations for an employee, he likely will assign engaging work tasks to the employee. In turn, the employee's self-esteem increases as does his confidence and on-the-job performance. Increased self-confidence contributes to the employee's motivation and willingness to accept future challenging assignments. In contrast, low expectations ensure the employee will remain unmotivated and will not perform as well as the employer expects. In addition, an employer who has low expectations in regards to an employee is less likely to provide the tools and equipment necessary for the employee to accomplish a work task, further diminishing the employee's motivation.

Lack of Interest in Subject Matter

An employee exhibits motivation as an interest or a driving force that persuades him to take action. An interested employee will be curious about a task and attempt to perform it well. Lack of interest can lead to decreased motivation and the failure to accomplish a goal. If an employee is not interested in particular tasks, he will not fully engage in his work. Instead, he will focus his attention elsewhere, not fully participate in the activity at hand and perform poorly.

Achievement Anxiety

Employees who experience achievement anxiety are sensitive to punishment, including criticism or the loss of something they value. As a result, achievement anxiety can inhibit employee behaviour. Anxious employees may be less interested in tasks and less motivated to achieve. For example, the employee may begin an activity but stop before he completes the task, if he becomes anxious about potential negative feedback.

Fear of Failure

If an employee fears failure, he fears a lack of success and will avoid work that he lacks the confidence to complete. The employee perceives a lack of success as a failure, which he believes is confirmation that he is flawed in some way. The more the employee fears failure, the less motivated he will be to perform work or attempt to accomplish goals because it is easier to avoid tasks than experiencing shame due to his failure to complete a task.

The framework of motivation indicates that motivation in a simple process. But in reality the task is more challenging:

1. The reason why motivation is a difficult task is that workforce is changing. Employees join an organisation with different needs and expectations.
2. Their values, beliefs, background, understanding, lifestyles, perception and attitudes are different.
3. It is difficult to design a common plan with the varied needs of the employees.
4. Motivating employees is more challenging at a time when organisations are following right-sizing or down-sizing.
5. It can also result in damaging the levels of trust and commitment.
6. Some organisations have resorted to hire and fire system.
7. Some organisations follow pay for performance.
8. Motives can only be inferred but not seen. What may work for one person may go the other way, for the other person.
9. It is very difficult to analyse what really motivates an individual and for how long.
10. Today the needs are diverse of employees and even the culture of the organisation is diverse.

5.2 Recent Trends and Problems in Retention

Employees are a valuable asset to any organisation. It is essential to protect this vital resource as talented and motivated employees play a crucial role in overall growth and success of the organisation. Retention of key employees is critical to the long-term health and success of any organisation. Focusing on employee retention techniques can positively impact the organisation as it increases employee productivity, performance, quality of work, profits, and reduces turnover and absenteeism.

Employee retention is a process in which the employees are encouraged to remain with the organisation for the maximum period of time or until the completion of the project. Effectively creating an engaging environment, recognising good performance, giving benefits and rewards, promoting mutual respect are some of the ways for effective employee retention.

Employee retention therefore refers to the ability of an organisation to retain its employees. Many consider employee retention as relating to the efforts by which employers attempt to retain employees in their workforce.

Employee retention is beneficial for the organisation as well as the employee. Employee retention matters as organisational issues such as training time and investment; lost knowledge; insecure employees and a costly candidate search are involved. Hence failing to retain a key employee is a costly proposition for an organisation. Various estimates suggest that losing a middle manager in most organisations costs up to five times of his salary. It is a known fact that retaining your best employees ensures customer satisfaction, increased product sales, satisfied colleagues and reporting staff, effective succession planning and deeply imbedded organisational knowledge and learning.

A distinction should be drawn between low performing employees and top performers and efforts to retain employees should be targeted at valuable and contributing employees. Employee turnover is a symptom of a deeper issue that has not been resolved. These deeper issues may include a low morale, absence of a clear career path, lack of recognition, poor employee-manager relationships or many other issues. Lack of satisfaction and commitment can also cause an employee to withdrawn and begin looking for other opportunities. Pay or money does not always play as large a role in inducing turnover as is typically believed.

It is important to pinpoint the root cause of the retention issue before implementing a programme to address it. A programme can be tailormade to meet the requirements of the organisation.

New Trends in Employee Retention Strategies

More and more businesses are using innovative "perks" that go beyond the traditional financial benefits characteristic of the past. Improved vacation allowances, gym memberships, pro-bono opportunities and family friendly policies are just some of the changes that are becoming vital in an increasingly competitive and dynamic market of recruiting and retaining legal talent.

In fact, many companies are now offering employees health, wellness and green incentives. This has proven beneficial to both the employee and employer.

Increasing Employee Engagement

Effectively implementing employee retention programmes by increasing employee engagement ensures that the employees are satisfied with their work, take pride in their work, report to duty on time, feel responsible for their job, feel valued for their contributions, and have high job satisfaction. As employees actively focus on their work, it increases the productivity levels in the organisation and leads to improvement in several associated areas. Employee engagement ensures that the employees have a clear understanding of their roles and responsibilities in the organisation. Increasing employee engagement helps to develop emotional connection, enthusiasm among the employees that promotes teamwork and healthy environment at the workplace.

Motivate Employees

Motivating employees by offering them better opportunities for career development can help in employee retention. Giving rewards, recognitions, promotions, and appreciation to employees can motivate them to increase their productivity, commitment to work, and loyalty to the organisation. They feel that their contributions are valued in the organisation. Giving incentives, pay hikes, bonuses can also help to motivate employees.

Recognising an employee's contributions and aspirations motivates employee to work productively and increases his confidence that helps in employee retention.

Focus on Team Building

Promoting team culture helps to actively involve all employees in achieving the goals and in overall success of the organisation. Promoting team building imbibes a sense of belongingness among the employees that they are a part of larger goals or objectives of the organisation. Team building promotes team work and team effort that help employees to tackle work pressure and thus provide a competitive advantage to the organisation.

Focusing on team building activities can help to reduce workplace conflicts between team members as they work in a team. Organising team building games, seminars, outdoor events help to promote team spirit, unity, and reduce stress.

Recognition of Performance

Recognition of performance of employees is an effective method of employee retention. Although monetary compensation can act as a motivating factor, openly recognising the performance, initiative, and good work increases the morale and motivates the employee to work more productively. Appreciating the performance motivates employees and they feel valuable within the organisation. This helps in employee engagement and to increase the productivity levels.

Fostering Employee Health and Wellness

Health and wellness trends are an exciting development in the employment market. Unlike traditional benefit plans which tend to focus on treating the illness, these new initiatives focus on the prevention of the illness in the first instance. In turn, these opportunities lead to positive consequences for the employer, through a happier, healthier and ideally more efficient workforce.

Personal Growth Opportunities

Another popular perk offered by employers is the facilitation and encouragement of personal growth opportunities. For example, many firms are increasingly placing value on providing high-quality learning and offering extensive professional development opportunities for employees, as well as encouraging public service work.

Green Initiatives

Firms are also beginning to set themselves apart by providing workplaces that encourage respect for the environment and foster green initiatives. In this case, helping the environment is not the only payoff, as green initiatives can also help attract new talent, increase productivity and reduce costs. Studies show that students coming out of school increasingly place value on workplaces that have less of a negative impact on the environment. Preliminary studies also link eco-friendly workplaces to higher productivity and less absenteeism.

Employee Retention Consultants

An employee retention consultant can assist organisations in the process of retaining top employees. Consultants can provide expertise on how to best identify the issue within an organisational that are related to turnover.

Join Stay Leave Model

For organisations and employers, understanding the environment is the first step to developing a long-term retention strategy. Organisations should understand why employees join, why they stay and why they leave an organisation.

Why Employees Join

The attractiveness of the position is usually what entices employees to join an organisation. High performing employees are more likely to retain when they are given realistic job previews. Organisations that attempt to oversell the position or company are only contributing to their own detriment when employees experience a discord between the position and what they were initially told. To assess and maintain retention, employers should mitigate any immediate conflicts of misunderstanding in order to prolong the employee's longevity with the organisation.

Why Employees Stay

Understanding why employees stay with an organisation is equally as important to understanding why employees choose to leave. Recent studies have suggested that as employees participate in their professional and community life, they develop a web of connections and relationships. These relationships prompt employees to become more embedded in their jobs and by leaving a job they would need to rearrange their social network.

Additionally the extent to which employees experience fit between themselves at their job, the lesser chance they will search elsewhere. A stay survey can help to take the pulse of an organisation's current work environment and the impact on their high performing employees.

Why Employees Leave

By understanding the reason behind why employees leave, organisations can better cater to their existing workforce and influence these decisions in the future. It is low satisfaction and commitment that initiates the withdrawal process, which includes thoughts of quitting in search of more attractive alternatives. If administered properly exit interviews can provide a great resource to why employees leave. The most common reasons for why employees leave are better pay, better hours and better opportunity. These typical answers for leaving often signal a much deeper issue that employers should investigate further into. Retention diagnostic is a rapid benchmarking process that identifies the costs and can help uncover what affects employee loyalty, performance and engagement.

Employee Retention Best Practices

By focusing on the fundamentals, organisations can go a long way towards building a high retention workplace. Organisations can start by defining their culture and identifying the types of individuals that would thrive in that environment. Attracting and recruiting top talent requires time, resources and capital. However there are all wasted if employees are not positioned to succeed within the company. Companies retain good employees by being employers of choice.

1. **Recruitment:** Presenting applicants with realistic job previews during the recruitment process have a positive effect on retaining new hires. Employers that are transparent about the positive and negative aspects of the job, as well as the challenges and expectations position themselves to recruit and retain stronger candidates

2. **Selection:** There are a variety of selection tools that can help predict job performance and subsequently retention. These include both subjective and objective methods of while organisations are accustomed to using more subjective tools such as interviews, application and resume evaluations, objective methods are increasing in popularity.

3. **Socialisation:** Socialisation practices delivered via a strategic on-boarding and assimilation programme can help new employees become embedded in the company and thus more likely to stay. Research has shown that socialisation practices can help new hires become embedded in the company and thus more likely to stay these practices include shared and individualised learning experiences, activities that allow people to get to know are another. Such practices may include providing employees with a role model, mentors or trainer or providing timely and adequate feedback.

4. **Training and Development:** Providing ample training and development opportunities can discourage turnover by keeping employees satisfied and well positioned for future growth opportunities. In fact dissatisfaction with potential career development is one of the top three reasons employees feel inclined to look elsewhere, if employees are not given opportunities to continually update their skills, they are more likely to leave. Those who receive training are less likely to quit than those who receive little or not training. Employers that fear providing training will make their employees more marketable and thus increase turnover can offer job specific training, which is less transferable to other contexts. Additionally employers can increase retention through development opportunities such as allowing employees is further their education and reimbursing tuition fees for employees who remain with the company for a specified amount of time.

5. **Compensation and Rewards:** Pay levels and satisfaction are only modest predictors of an employee's decision to leave the organisation, however organisations can lead the market with a strong compensation and reward package. Organisations can explicitly link rewards to retention (i.e., vacation hours to seniority, offer retention bonuses to stock options or define benefit plan payouts to years of services). Research has shown that well defined compensation package and rewards as associated with longer tenure.

6. **Effective Leaders:** An employee's relationship with his supervisor and manager is equally important to keeping to making an employee feel embedded and valued within the organisation. Supervisors need to understand as to how to motivate their employees and reduce cost while building loyalty in their key people. Managers need to reinforce employee productivity and open communication to coach employees and provide meaningful feedback and inspire employees and provide meaningful feedback and inspire employees to work as an effective team. In order to achieve this, organisation need to prepare managers and supervisors to lead and develop effective relationships with their subordinates.

Executive coaching can help increase an individual's effectiveness as a leader as well as boost a climate of learning, trust and teamwork in an organisation to encourage supervisors to focus on retention among their teams, organisations can incorporate retention metric into their organisations evaluation.

7. Employee Engagement: Employees who are satisfied with their jobs enjoy their work of the organisation, believe their job to be more important, take pride in the company and feel their contributions are impactful, are five times less likely to quit than employees who were not engaged. Engaged employees give their companies crucial competitive advantages including higher productivity and lower employee turnover.

Retaining employees has always proved to be fruitful across many industries rather than to search for new and efficient talent. So to gain the fruit of this tree, different companies devise different strategies for retaining their employees, simply hiking ones salary in an endeavor to retain your valuable employee will serve no purpose as today's workforce has a lot going during his/her decision-making process and ill certainly not restricted to just pay.

5.3 Recent Trends and Problems in Attrition

Attrition in human resource terminology refers to the phenomenon of the employees leaving the company. It is usually measured with a metric called attrition rate, which simply measures the number of employees moving out of the company. It is also referred as churn rate or turnover.

Attrition simply means *"A reduction in the number of employees through retirement, resignation or death."*

Attrition in human resources thus refers to the gradual loss of employees over time. In general, relatively high attrition is problematic for companies. HR professionals often assume a leadership role in designing company compensation programmes, work culture and motivation systems that help the organisation retain top employees.

The meaning of attrition in a work environment refers to a reduction or decrease in the size or strength the work force, or a gradual reduction in labour occurring through means other than firing employees. Both of these explanations can be applied to activities addressed by human resources, and both can have positive and negative ramifications for a company. Human resources teams factor attrition rates into their department budgets to account for potential losses in productivity and the costs associated with replacing departing employees.

A major problem in high employee attrition is its cost to an organisation. Job postings, hiring processes, paperwork and new hire training are some of the common expenses of losing employees and replacing them. Additionally, regular employee turnover prohibits your organisation from increasing its collective knowledge base and experience over time. This is especially concerning if your business is customer facing, as customers often prefer to interact with familiar people. Errors and issues are more likely if you constantly have new workers.

Reasons for Attrition

Attrition can be encouraged when it is part of a strategic business manoeuvre to reduce costs. It can also manifest itself when employees voluntarily leave their jobs. This can happen for a variety of reasons: employees may move or retire, take another job, be ill-suited to the position they were hired to fill, or want employment that offers a more equitable work-life balance. Others may experience a lack of the freedom or autonomy they require to perform at expected levels. Human resources professionals inadvertently encourage attrition when they disregard or ignore maltreatment of employees by management.

Common reasons experienced by HR manager are as follows:

1. Insufficient remuneration and employee benefits paid to employee by his employer.
2. Mismatch of job profile.
3. Job stress and work
4. Odd working hours.
5. Early morning, night shifts.
6. Entering of new companies and sectors into the market.
7. Lack of authority provided to accomplish one task.
8. Monotony of job.
9. Lack of proper environment.
10. Poor concern about employees by their employer.
11. Poor promotion policies or lack of promotion for long time.

The list is endless but the reason why employees leave the organisation varies according to the nature of the business. The work should give to them the level of the employees and the nature of the responsibility he/she can handle. Therefore it's a very challenge task for an HR expert to cope up with this situation and retain talent with an organisation.

Associated Costs with High Attrition

1. **Talent Loss:** It includes the cost of lost knowledge, skills and contacts that the person who is leaving is taking with them out of your door.
2. **Recruitment Cost:**
   - The cost of advertisements, agency costs, employee referral costs, internet posting costs.
   - Calculate the cost of the manager who has to understand what work remains, and how to cover that work until a replacement is found.
   - Cost of the various candidate pre-employment tests to help assess candidate's skills, abilities, aptitude, attitude, value and behaviours.

3. **Training Cost:**
   - It includes the cost of orientation in terms of the new person's salary and the cost of the person who conducts the orientation.
   - It also consists of the training.
   - Calculate the cost of various training materials needed including company product manuals, computer or other technology equipment used in the delivery of the training.
4. **Motivational Cost:**
   - It refers to the cost arises because of motivating the other employees to retain them in the organisation in terms of increasing their salary and time.
5. **Low Productivity Cost:**
   - As the new employee is learning the new job, the company policies and practices etc., they are not fully productive.

Concerns for HR

Employee Retention is the biggest challenge faced by HR in the modern economy. The best retention strategies are to be framed to curb the attrition. Hiring and employee retention have been identified as the 'key challenges' in managing and measuring employee productivity.

Changing Hiring Practices

Hiring practices have undergone a transformational change to build the loyalty and commitment among the employees. Recruitment involves a systematic procedure for hiring the valuable employees. HR has to develop policies based on trust, openness, equity and consensus with creating an environment where people are willing to work with zeal, initiative and passion and there should be no misfit between the job skill and employee skills. Recruiting and retention are interconnected. When a company is trying to "retain" talent, it is in fact "attracting" talent as well.

Employer Branding

In the modern economy of cut throat competition the buzz word employee branding a strategic tool to retain the employees. Employer branding is about building the positive image of the organisation in the minds of the employees as a dream place to work. As it helps to attract and retain talent in the era of employee attrition.

Talent Management

The greatest challenge faced by HR is to successfully attract, assess, train and retain employees. HR specialist has to attract the right resources and retain talented resources. Talent management involves processes adopted by companies come to realise that their employees' talents and skills drive their business success. Innovative talent strategies should be reworked and streamlined by HR managers to identify and develop talent to retain the employees in the organisation.

Employee Engagement

An engaged employee is one who is fully involved in his or her work, and thus will act in a way that furthers their organisation's interests. Engaged employees speaks positively about the organisation to co-workers, potential employees and customers, having a strong desire to be a member of the organisation, and exerting extra effort to contribute to the organisation's success. Many smart organisations work to develop and nurture engagement. Employee engagement is critical to any organisation that seeks not only to retain valued employees, but also increase its level of performance.

Exit Interview

Exit interviews are conducted by most of the organisations. Exit interviews are used as catalyst for identifying the reasons for employee attrition. Exit interviews should be properly organised so that employee turnover can be reduced and increase the retention.

In this heightened corporate oversight HR is expected to face the challenge of employee attrition by implementing effective retention strategies to retain the employees in the organisation and contribute to the winning edge of the organisation. Relying on the traditional sources like infrastructure, technology, money etc. organisation excellence cannot be achieved. More and more organisations are realizing that people are central to an organisations excellence.

Organisations has to built great workforce in terms of work culture, environment and practices so that employees come next day with same energy, enthusiasm and zeal and retain in the organisation.

5.4 Downsizing

Downsizing occurs when a company permanently reduces its workforce. Corporate downsizing is often the result of poor economic conditions and the company's need to cut jobs in order to lower costs or maintain profitability.

Downsizing is thus a term for reducing the size of the employment force to reduce costs. If implemented and managed correctly, employers can be successful in shrinking the size of the employment force while also reducing costs. However, HR has a crucial role in ensuring that the remaining workforce maintains its level of productivity and morale.

Downsizing may occur when one company merges with another, a product or service is cut or the economy falters. Downsizing also occurs when employers want to "streamline" a company this refers to corporate restructuring in order to increase profit and maximise efficiency.

Downsizing refers to the reduction of a company's labour force. Instead of firing workers, however the employer shrinks the payroll by permanently eliminating positions. This approach has gained popularity since the 1980's for companies looking to cut costs during tough economic times or to improve efficiency and performance. Some employers may also be cutting employees hours, or instituting unpaid vacation days as less devastating alternatives. Over the last few years, we have seen plenty of companies downsizing due to the rough economy. In a normal economic cycle, companies cut jobs when the economy is in recession mode and adds job when the economy is growing.

Downsizing results in layoffs that are often followed by other restructuring changes, such as branch closings, departmental consolidation and other forms of cutting pay expenses. In some cases employers are not fired, but instead become part time or temporary workers.

Downsizing Decision

Human resource managers should weigh in on several factors that influence downsizing decisions. First, identify the specific problems downsizing is expected to solve and then assess the resources that can be devoted to it right now. Also consider how downsizing will affect the company in the longer term. For example, the manager must determine if and how strong performers with unique skills be replaced when things improve, and what risks are involved in losing those individuals.

Businesses use several techniques in downsizing, including providing incentives to take early retirement and transfer to subsidiary companies, but the most common technique is to simply terminate the employment of a certain number of people.

Employment downsizing has become a fact of working life as companies struggle to cut costs and adapt to changing market demands.

Trends

Downsizing is typically intended as a cost-saving measure; however, it may not always be successful. Remaining employees may be forced to work overtime and outgoing employees may pursue grievances against the employer, undermining the employer's goal in reducing the size of its workforce. Thus, the trend is to treat downsizing or layoffs as an absolute last resort, particularly where other types of cost-saving measures are available like reducing employee hours, work-sharing programs, employee education and employee relocation.

If downsizing absolutely cannot be avoided, HR's objective should be to maintain productivity and morale following downsizing and use alternative dispute resolution measures to address outgoing employee grievances before they get out of hand.

5.5 Manpower Outsourcing

Concept of Manpower Outsourcing

In outsourcing, an external firm or company carries on management of a product on behalf of another firm. The concept started when companies were reluctant to hire new employees for short-term jobs. Hiring new employees means more work for the people, security check and other overheads, which was not a worthy undertaking for a small project.

Manpower outsourcing answered this problem, as in this case the primary company doesn't hire the worker directly; the external firms who supply the skilled workers are called manpower outsourcing firms.

Manpower outsourcing is required when a firm needs to complete a task in which they don't want to hire new employees. Outsourcing is an efficient way to save cost. Currently many information technology (IT) firms and call centers rely on outsourcing.

Outsourcing allows companies to focus on other business while the manpower staffing provider recruits, supplies and manages the staff for them.

Lack of skilled workers is another scenario when, manpower outsourcing is required. Many IT firms at times require people well-versed in specific technology which they might not otherwise, have in their resource pool. In such cases they can hire skilled professionals called consultants to complete their task.

Manpower Outsourcing Procedure

Once a company decides upon outsourcing, they look for an appropriate supplier and ask for Request for Proposal (RFP). Sometimes RFPs from multiple vendors are requested. In RFP, vendors cover the process that they will follow to complete the project, current financial position of the company, technical ability of its employees and all the information, which can help win over the confidence of the company. Then the company negotiates with companies and decides on their best and final offer.

Both the parties finalise the contract and sign it. The next step is the transition of knowledge and information from the source company to the company providing manpower. Delivery schedule is decided for the delivery of the product. Once the project is finished, the source company can decide to terminate the contract or may renew the contract.

Why Outsource Manpower?

Some of the benefits of outsourcing are listed below:
1. First and by far the most important aspect is cost reduction of development of overall project.
2. Hiring manpower from an outsource company who has good and knowledgeable skilled professionals in the field, can improve quality of the product.
3. Lowering pressure on HR department of hiring and maintaining skilled professionals.
4. Companies can put more emphasis on designing and research of a product rather putting effort on meeting deadlines.

Disadvantages of Outsourcing

Some of the disadvantages of outsourcing are:
1. Manpower outsourcing can impact workers or employees of the company. Sometimes companies cut jobs in their companies and outsource the work to a third party.

2. Most often outsourcing companies are not able to meet the standards and timelines.
3. There are also concern related to fraud and security, as there is always a chance of identity theft or misuse of sensitive information.

Companies today complete to sustain their clients and yet provide a quality service. The only way they can survive is by reducing their running cost. It is one of the best and most efficient ways to reduce the cost of development of a project. The contracting or subcontracting of non-core activities to free-up cash, personnel, time and facilities for activities in which a company holds competitive advantage. Companies have strength in other areas may contract out data processing, legal, manufacturing marketing, payroll accounting or other aspects of their business to concentrate on what they do best is often an integral part of downsizing or reengineering.

5.6 International Human Resource Management (IHRM)

Definitions of IHRM

IHRM can be defined as *a set of activities aimed at managing organisational human resources at international level to achieve organisational objectives and achieve competitive advantage over competitors at national and international level.*

IHRM includes typical HRM functions such as recruitment, selection, training and development, performance appraisal and dismissal done at international level and additional activities such as global skills management, expatriate management and so on.

In simple terms, IHRM is concerned about managing human resources at Multinational Companies (MNC) and it involves managing three types of employees namely,

Home country employees: Employees belonging to home country of the firm where the corporate head quarter is situated.

Host country employees: Employees belonging to the nation in which the subsidiary is situated.

Third country employees: These are the employees who are not from home country/host country but are employed at subsidiary or corporate head quarters. As an example an American MNC which has a subsidiary at India may employ a French person as the CEO to the subsidiary. The Frenchman employed is a third country employee.

IHRM is therefore defined as *performing HRM and its related activities and arranging for related and necessary cultural and immigration facilities for prospective and current employees, by organisations operating in domestic and foreign countries.*

It is clear that IHRM deals with all functions of HRM in addition to performing other functions exclusively for expatriates. Certain additional functions like resolving the disputes between domestic and foreign employees are also to be performed under IHRM.

P. Morgan defines IHRM as *the interplay among human resource activities, types of employees and countries.*

IHRM is *the process of procuring, allocating and effectively utilising human resources in a multinational corporation.* A multinational corporation is defined as an enterprise that has an interlocking network of subsidiaries in several countries. IHRM is about the worldwide management of Human resources. The purpose of IHRM is to enable the firm the multi-national enterprise to be successful globally. This emphasis on its part to be:

(a) Competitive through the world.
(b) Efficient.
(c) Locally responsive.
(d) Flexible and adaptable within the shortest of the period.
(e) Capable of transferring learning across their globally dispersed units.

The growing importance of multinational enterprises and the use of complex global business decisions have generated a linkage of IHRM with the strategic needs of the business and developed a strategic prospective of IHRM. IHRM policies and practices relevant to the needs of MNEs (Multinational Enterprise) include those related to planning, staffing, appraising compensating, training and developing and labour relations. Human resource managers in MNCs must integrate human resource policies and practices across a number of subsidiaries in different countries so that overall corporate objectives can be achieved.

Differences between Domestic HRM and International HRM (IHRM) are summarised below:

- Domestic HRM is done at the national level and IHRM is done at the international level.
- Domestic HRM is concerned with managing employees belonging to one nation and IHRM is concerned with managing employees belonging to many nations (Home country, host country and third country employees)
- Domestic HRM is concerned with managing limited number of HRM activities at national level and IHRM has concerned with managing additional activities such as expatriate management.
- Domestic HRM is less complicated due to less influence from the external environment. IHRM is very complicated as it is affected heavily by external factors such as cultural distance and institutional factors.

Dimensions of IHRM

According to P.V. Morgan: IHRM is the interplay among 3 dimensions:
- HR Activities
- Types of employees
- Types of Countries

Objectives of IHRM
- Remaining competitive throughout the world
- Efficient
- Locally Responsive
- Flexible and adaptive
- Capable to transforming learning across their globally dispersed units

Role of International HRM

International human resource management is the basis of success of any global multinational organisation. International HRM enhances employee's effectiveness to achieve goals of the organisation and meet the needs; to develop employees to assume more diverse tasks, assignments, face challenging situations and better understand the cultural variations across the nations.

IHRM Functions

1. **Planning:** Human resource planning is pivotal to the successful operation of a MNC. Planning in MNCs is essential for the efficient use of human resources. HR planning should effectively synchronise the staffing, appraisal, and compensation subsystems of IHRM. Such planning must be comprehensive in scope and responsive to the MNE's characteristics.

2. **Hiring:** A subsidiary HR manager should use a hiring process that fits the local labour market. It is important to invest considerable time and effort in the selection process and to provide increased training to local employees when they take up the job. Appropriate training materials have to be prepared and methodology has to be followed across culture.

3. **Staffing:** Staffing is a major IHRM practice that MNE's need to open their recruitment process to enhance the attractiveness of global assignments.

4. **Appraising Performance:** Culture helps to determine what aspects of performance should be appraised and how that appraisal should be conducted. The development of performance appraisal systems for use with expatriates requires extreme care. The active involvement of the expatriate, home country supervisors and host country supervisors is often important. While the expatriate is on assignment the individual performance must be appraised. For the expatriate, in contrast to domestic MNE's need to evaluate dimension of performance not specifically job related such as cross-culture interpersonal qualities, sensitivity the foreign norms, laws and customs and adaptability to uncertain and unpredictable conditions.

5. **Compensation Systems:** Compensation polices with each subsidiary must be consistent with the local market, wage legislation and regulations, union influences and cultural preferences. The subsidiary compensation system must provide an adequate level of strategic consistency within the MNC's overall business strategy. The subsidiary HR manager must deal with a separate system applicable to home country expatriates and third country national working for the subsidiary.

   There are a variety of factors that affect compensation systems within MNC's. MNC compensation systems are influenced by internal business factors such as varying wage costs, levels of job security and differing business strategies.

   Most expatriate compensation plans are designed to achieve four important objectives:
   (i) Attract employees who are qualified and interested in international assignments.
   (ii) Facilitate the movement of expatriates from one subsidiary to another from home to subsidiaries and from subsidiaries back home.
   (iii) Provide a consistent and reasonable relationship between the pay levels of employees at headquarters domestic affiliates and foreign subsidiaries.
   (iv) Be cost effective by reducing unnecessary expenses.

6. **Training:** To maximise training efficiency, the international HR manager should select and develop training programmes that best fit the particular assignment and individual.

   The different aspects to be considered in selecting the type of training programmes are:
   (i) Business strategy.
   (ii) Job requirements.
   (iii) Cultural similarities and dissimilarities.
   (iv) Communication with local nationals.

IHRM policies and practices may strengthen inter unit linkages in numerous ways, including:
(a) Comprehensive human resource planning, ensuring that the MNE has the appropriate people in place around the world at the right time.
(b) Staff policies that capitalise on the worldwide expertise of expatriates and host country nationals.
(c) Performance appraisals that are anchored in the competitive strategies of Multinational Enterprise (MNE) headquarters and host units.
(d) Compensation policies those are strategically and culturally relevant.
(e) Training and development initiatives that prepare individuals to operate effectively in their overseas locations and to cooperate with other MNE units.

Comparison between International Human Resource Management and Domestic Human Resource Management

In a wider sense IHRM involves the same activities as domestic HRM. Domestic HRM is involved with employees within one national boundary only. HR managers working in a domestic environment generally administer programmes for a single national group of employee who are covered with a Uniform Compensation policy. Domestic HRM is performing HRM functions in a domestic organisation which employs exclusively nationals of that particular field in which it is located and operating.

HR managers working in an international environment face the problem of designing and administering programmes for more than one national group of employees. The HR department needs demands that the expatriate employee understands housing arrangements, health care and all aspects of the compensation package provided for the assignment.

Major external factors that influence international HRM are the type of government, the state of the economy and the generally accepted practices of doing business in each of the various host countries in which the multinational operates. International business involves the interaction and movement of people across national boundaries and appreciation of cultural differences and when these differences are important and essential.

In IHRM or domestic HRM hiring of placing people in positions where they can perform effectively is a goal of most organisations. Technical competencies are necessary but not sufficient condition for successful performance of international management positions.

Cross-cultural interpersonal skills sensitivity to foreign norms and values, and case of adaptation to unfamiliar environments are just a few of the managerial characteristics when selecting international managers.

An effective performance management system also has to deal with the challenges of comparing subsidiary managers in different countries. The question for the multinational firm is how to maintain and leverage its human resources to that suitably trained internationally oriented personnel are available to support its strategic responses and contribute to its core competencies.

Training and development programmes are an integral part of an effective performance management system. Training aims to improve current work skills and behaviour whereas development aims to increase abilities in relation to some future position or job usually managerial. For multinational firms, successful management of compensation and benefits requires knowledge of the employment of taxation laws, customs, environment and employment practices of many foreign countries. Also needed are familiarity with currency fluctuations and the effect of inflation on compensation and an understanding of which allowances must be granted and which allowances are necessary in which country. All of these needs must be fulfilled within the context of shifting political, economic and social conditions. Because of their high cost, HR manager spend a great deal of time developing effective compensation and benefit programmes for international employees.

While preparing international compensation policies a firm seeks to satisfy several objectives. First, the policy should be consistent with the overall strategy, structure and business needs of the multinational. Secondly, the policy must work to attract and retain staff in the areas where the multinational has the greatest needs of opportunities. Thirdly, the policy should give due consideration to equity and sound implementation. The key components of international compensation include base salary, Foreign Service inducement allowance and benefits. Multinational firms need to match their compensation policies with their staffing policies and general HR philosophy. In international labour relations, it is important to realise that it is difficult to compare, industrial relations systems and behaviour across national boundaries.

IHRM deals with the employees from a number of nations in contrast to domestic HRM where employees are drawn from one nation. People from different nations come with a variety of culture, values and ethical interpretations. Cultures and behaviour of people vary based on geographical regions.

An organisation seeks the information on broader aspects of employees and their family members while recruiting and selecting employees from foreign countries. These aspects include, age, health, educational qualifications, driving skills criminal record of employee and his family members. International employees need to be provided security facilities in case of wars, riots, hostage and other such situations.

International environment has become complex, highly competitive, dynamic, vibrant, interlined and interdependent. Human resources can stay in their home country and work for a company located in foreign country via internet and other modes of information technology. This process does not reduce the role of IHRM. In contrast it enhances the role of IHRM and yet complicates the IHRM process as employees need to be managed by a blend of HRM practices prevailing in both the countries.

In addition information technology allows location of manufacturing centers in various countries with the help of computer aided manufacturing techniques thus creating employment opportunities in various countries.

The shifts in political ideologies of various countries along with globalisation are note worthy. Political rules and regulations of various governments are significantly liberalised. The domestic HRM practices are mostly influenced by the domestic economic, political, technical and social factor while IHRM is influenced by environmental factors of host country.

5.7 Multiculturism/Multiculturalism

The globalisation of business, increased mobility of labour across geographic borders is leading to multiculturalism among several countries. For example, in countries such as Canada, US, UK, India, and Australia, multiculturalism is increasingly becoming an integral part of the national identity. In addition, cross-border mergers and acquisitions (e.g. Arcelor-Mittal) and deployment of teams for certain projects, require organisations to draw from a pool of human resources from different countries.

The globalisation of the business environment that is being driven by technological and economic factors is resulting in an ever-increasing number of cross-cultural interactions in the workplace.

Recent estimates indicate that there are over 1000,000 firms with international operations, and they have annual revenues in excess of $3500 billion. Not surprisingly, the growth in the number of firms with international operations has been accompanied by an increase in the cultural diversity of their employees.

Much of our personal and interpersonal interactions are guided by cultural values, expectations, and attitudes. Some values transcend cultural boundaries and are mutually reinforcing. Other cultural values create interactions with high potential for conflict, misunderstanding, poor performance, and ultimately, individual and organisational ineffectiveness or failure.

The Oxford Dictionary defines the word multicultural as *'including of people of several different races, religions, languages and traditions'.*

Multiculturalism is defined *as the presence of people from two or more cultural backgrounds within an organisation.*

Multicultural work force is one *wherein a company's employees include members of a variety of ethnic, racial, religious, and gender backgrounds whereas managing multicultural workforce goes further, and focuses on changing mindsets, organisation culture. It's strategy-driven and is seen as contributing to the organisational goals of profit, productivity and morale.*

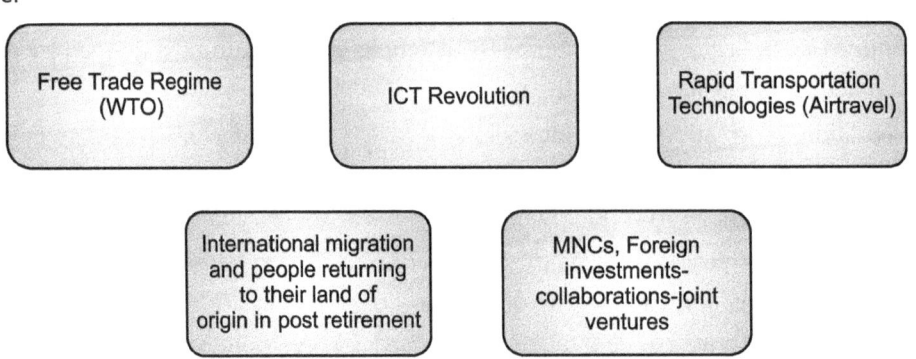

Fig 5.1: Sources of Multiculturalism

The multiculturalism in Indian firms may lead to substantial benefits, including increased creativity, improved decision making, and broader markets for products. However, more cultural diversity also may pose important challenges for these firms, whether or not they have multinational operations. For instance, as cultural diversity increases, firms may need to develop new strategies for managing and motivating their employees. Other cultural values create interactions with high potential for conflict, misunderstanding, poor performance, and ultimately, individual and organisational ineffectiveness or failure. Such problems are influencing HR practices in many organisations.

Many companies have culturally diverse workforces. This applies to medium- and small-sized businesses as well as to multinational organisations. The existence of a multicultural workforce has important implications for human resource management policies. The Management of a Multicultural Workforce takes a systematic approach to relating organisational features and activities to specific aspects of national culture.

Multiculturalism is an indisputable fact of life in today's world. However, managing multiculturalism is indeed a challenge both at the, governance as well as managerial levels. Organisations are increasingly realising vast diversity within the global market and devising strategies to make the most out of it.

Benefits of a multicultural workforce

- Companies that create diversity in the workplace are generally more profitable and successful than those who don't.
- The most successful companies are those that recognise the power of diversity in their workforce. They can effectively create products and services that appeal to their increasingly diverse customer bases. These companies know that diversity will become even more important as markets get integrated, hence they would attempt to very well reflect diversity value to the marketplaces they serve.
- Further, cross-cultural teamwork and collaboration are essential, if people are to function productively, they must learn to see their differences as assets, rather than as liabilities.
- When an organisation understands and honours multiculturalism, a bond forms between employer and employee.
- Marketing opportunities increase exponentially.
- Creativity and innovation are stimulated, it inspires high level of creativity and promotes innovation in the workplace.
- Business image is enhanced and extended beyond traditional borders.
- Skill and talent can be attracted from diverse cultures and organisations can retain the best available human talent, and develop new markets.
- It gives a competitive edge.

- Synchronisation in workplace and high turnout. Interpersonal-teamwork, problem solving.
- Personal-employee morale, career growth, professional development, increased productivity.
- When there is no diversity, it constrains thinking. Differing viewpoints enrich the workplace. It doesn't diminish. It enhances the competitive advantage of a company.

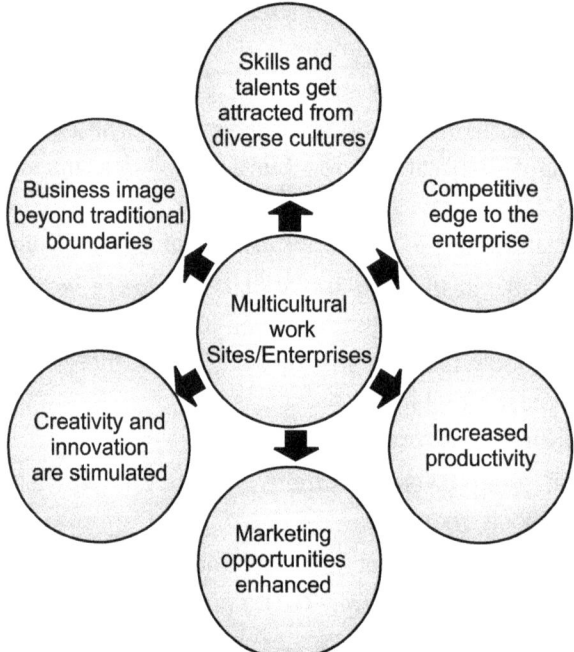

Fig 5.2: Benefits of a Multicultural Workforce

The skills needed for managing people from diverse backgrounds at work or outside the work place can be very different because in the workplace we are in our work roles and there are many external constraints to our behaviour. Many people actually spend more time awake with their colleagues than with their spouse and children. So any problems arising in this area will definitely spill over onto the private life.

Looking carefully into the factors that affect multicultural team leadership or management, we can identify five factors that operate at team levels.

1. National culture
2. Corporate culture of the organisation
3. Nature of the industry
4. Stage of team development
5. Personal attributes.

1. **National Culture**

   There are ample theories and much research into how national cultures affect team behaviour. National culture has many dimensions like orientation to time, style of communication, personal space, competitiveness and worldview. Generally we are dealing with stereotypes and cultural biases here. Regional and personal life experience traits can override these ascribed 'national' culture traits.

2. **Corporate Culture**

   Corporate culture is very closely related to the functional culture and it is a result of a historical process where the founder and successive leaders have left their marks. A large multinational organisation is bound to have a more structured, hierarchic and bureaucratic approach to running its affairs while an internet web design company with young creative artists would be an entirely different environment.

3. **Nature of the Industry**

   Coal miners, web designers and international bankers would seem to come from different worlds dress, language, etiquette, unwritten codes of behaviour accepted practice and skills needed on the job vary to a great extent in different industries. It is of vital importance that the industry, the organisation or the environment allows team members to display a sense of pride in one's professional identity.

4. **Stage of Team Development**

   If the team is just recently formed with no history or experience the rules of the game have to be learnt by everyone. If the team has a history of performing efficiently, new entrants can rely on established practice and older members to teach them the skills required. The stage of development of the team member also plays a great role here. If the team is in the formation stage, the rules of the game are still being negotiated and people are learning their own roles.

5. **Personal Attributes**

   Last but not least is all the other factors like personality, competence profile, the individuals own life experience, expectations of rewards, acknowledgement and satisfaction from working in the team as well as previous history of team working.

   The first three factors are static factors, which mean that their characteristics cannot be easily changed by individual action. Team members or even the whole team cannot change the national culture. Individuals, teams and organisations have to learn to adapt to them. In fact the efficiency of the team is directly correlated to how well this adaptation has been achieved. But intervention can greatly affect the last two factors of stages of Team Development and Personal Attributes.

A team can accelerate its progress from formation stage to the stage of maturity and an individual can change personal attributes by acquiring new competences. Superior sustainable team performance can be achieved only if team members learn to take into account dimensions of national culture like orientation to time, style of communication, personal space, competitions and worldview and have successfully adapted their working practice to reflect the team member's background realities.

5.8 Cross Cultural Training (CCT)

The term **Cross Cultural Training** refers to a variety of different training courses. Each in essence aims to develop awareness between people where a common cultural framework does not exist.

Cross cultural training in general can be defined as *"Any intervention aimed at increasing an individual's capability to cope with work in foreign environment"*.

Cross cultural training is defined as *any planned intervention designed to increase the knowledge and skills of expatriates to live and work efficiently and achieve general life satisfaction in an unfamiliar host culture.*

In general cross cultural training has two parallel approaches.
1. General/Cross Cultural Awareness Training and
2. Culture/Country Specific Training.

Need and Importance of Cross Cultural Training

Cross Cultural Training (CCT) has become an increasingly important human resource development activity due to the surge of globalisation. The need for cross cultural capabilities has become crucial to conduct international business. Organisations are challenged to compete in global market. Often, corporations have to provide appropriate cross cultural training for expatriates and their families for foreign assignments.

Some of the benefits of cross cultural training are as follows:
- Culturally confident employees are more effective and productive.
- Training reduces incidents of cultural shock for employees and their families.
- Culturally aware employees are more effective in leadership roles and managing multicultural teams.
- Cultural awareness is the key to building successful relationships.
- Training is an effective way to minimise breakdowns in communication, costly misunderstandings and business blunders.
- Culturally aware employees are effective communicators and valuable company ambassadors.
- Cross-cultural training is an investment that will pay long-term dividends.
- Companies providing cross-cultural training have a competitive advantage over their competition.

Cross cultural awareness training deals with the manifestations of culture in the workplace and has many applications. Its main purpose is to evaluate and constructively tackle the challenges cross cultural differences can bring to workplace.

Cross cultural team building training will aim to raise team members' awareness of each other culturally in order to foster mutual trust, respect and understanding. The result of which will be clearer lines of communication.

Cross cultural management training aims to equip management staff with the knowledge and skills to effectively supervise a multi-cultural staff cross cultural awareness training results in a more convivial and understanding work environment.

Cross cultural negotiation training assists negotiators involved with foreign clients or customers with whom they are discussing possible terms and conditions.

Cultural diversity training offers HR staff support in helping them understand their responsibilities to ethnic minority staff or look at ways of nurturing harmonious interpersonal relationships at work.

Culture specific training is generally aimed at individuals or teams that regularly visit a foreign country or who frequently interact with overseas clients or colleagues. Such training usually focuses on areas such as values, morals, ethics, business practices, etiquette, protocol or negotiation styles with reference to one country. This better equips participants with the key skills that will help in building successful business relationships. Different approaches can be used to train and raise intercultural awareness.

The different types of cross-cultural training are as follows:

1. **Attribution training:** In this type of training, employees in an international environment try to interpret behaviour from the viewpoint of nationals from the host culture.
2. **Culture awareness training:** This method of training makes use of cultural sensitivity training groups to explore the expatriate's culture of origin. The assumption is that through understanding one's own biases and values, expatriates understand better the dynamics of intercultural communication.
3. **Interaction training:** This method involves on the job training where the expatriate employee learns the basics from an experienced and established expatriate.
4. **Didactic training:** This method of training is to provide the expatriate with practical information and facts regarding living conditions, cultural differences, job details etc.
5. **Experiential training:** This type of intercultural training uses simulations, role plays and visits to the host country.
6. **Language training:** Language acquisition plays an important role in understanding a new culture and adjusting to it. However, one should make a clear distinction between linguistic skills and intercultural skills.

A good cross-cultural programme should focus on these elements:
1. Management styles and culture.
2. How sources of motivation can greatly vary from culture to culture.
3. How supervision styles favoured in one culture can be catastrophic in another.
4. How hierarchy is perceived differently and what that means when conducting meetings or brainstorming sessions.
5. What is the place of interpersonal relationships in business?

Communication Styles

Another important area of focus is communication styles. Communication is not merely a matter of language rather it understands the intention behind the words. Across cultures this becomes more complex, as some value direct communication styles while others, preoccupied with harmony, honour, or hierarchy will often prefer an indirect style. This is when that's not possible 'we will see'. How long does it take an unprepared employee overseas to understand that 'yes, yes' simply means 'I acknowledge that you are talking to me or that the answer to do you understand' will always be 'yes'.

An effective cross cultural training should also take into account the company's culture and whether the company wishes to establish its culture in the overseas location or whether it accepts to adjust to local culture. For example, is management local? does it view itself as a multinational company? etc.

Training Methods

A variety of training methodologies are available for CCT. In Table 5.1, we outline some of the popular ones and give a brief description of each.

Table 5.1: Cross Cultural Training Methods (Francesco, Gold, 1998)

Cultural Briefings	Explain the major aspects of the host country culture, including customs, traditions, everyday behaviors.
Area Briefings	Explain the history, geography, economy, politics and other general information about the host country and region.
Cases	Portray a real life situation in business or personal life to illustrate some aspect of living or working in the host culture.
Role Playing	Allows the trainee to act out a situation that he or she might face in living or working in the host country.
Culture Assimilator	Provides a written set of situations that the trainee might encounter in living or working in the host country.
Field Experiences	Provide an opportunity for the trainee to go to the host country or another unfamiliar culture to experience living and working there for a short time.

5.9 New Terms

1. **HCN - Host Country National:** HCN is defined as *'an employee to be hired who is a citizen of the nation in which the subsidiary is operating, which is different from the parent company's home nation'*.

2. **PCN - Home Country National (Parent Community National):** 'PCN' is defined as *'an employee to be sent abroad who is a citizen of the nation in which the subsidiary is operating, which is different from the parent company's home nation.'*

3. **TCN - Third Country National:** TCN is defined as *'an employee who will be sent to another nation to work who is a citizen of neither the parent company nation or the host country nations'*.

4. **Ethnocentric Approach:** Hiring and promoting employees on the basis of parent company's home country frame of reference. Companies with primarily international strategic orientation (characterised by low pressures for cost reduction and low pressures for local responsiveness) may adopt for an ethnocentric approach. In this approach most decisions are made of headquarters using the home country's frame of reference. Hence, most of the experts are 'home-country nationals' or 'parent company national'. Often, some of these people have a hard time adapting nationals are often hired for an international assignment because there are no suitable host country nationals available.

5. **Polycentric Approach:** Hiring and promoting employees on the basis of the specific local context in which the subsidiary operates which implies the primary strategic orientation is "multi-domestic" meaning low pressures for cost reduction, but high pressures for local responsiveness and product adaptation. In this case companies tend to hire more 'host country nationals' (HCN's), a citizen of the nation in which the subsidiary is operating, while limiting the number of the PCN's in the subsidiary and keeping them for home office management. When host country nationals are employed they are familiar with local customs, culture and the language.

6. **Geocentric Approach:** Hiring and promoting employees on the basis of ability and experience without considering race or citizenship and usually this implies a high pressure for both cost responsiveness and local responsiveness, for example, transnational companies. Indeed, the transnational companies hire many TCN's as they are looking for the best qualified person to take a job in a particular country.

POINTS TO REMEMBER

- Human resource management (HRM) has always been a very challenging aspect of any business. Especially with so much happening in the world of Human Resource, change, indeed is the constant when we talk about Human resource management.
- **Motivation** is the set of forces that cause people to behave in certain ways.
- Today is an extremely dynamic and volatile work environment marked by continued turbulence in the economy. Managers face a difficult challenge of motivating and retaining employees in an environment of increased uncertainties.
- Retention of key employees is critical to the long-term health and success of any organisation. Employee **retention** is a process in which the employees are encouraged to remain with the organisation for the maximum period of time or until the completion of the project.
- More and more businesses are using innovative "perks" that go beyond the traditional financial benefits characteristic of the past. Improved vacation allowances, gym memberships, pro-bono opportunities and family friendly policies are just some of the changes that are becoming vital in an increasingly competitive and dynamic market of recruiting and retaining legal talent.
- **Attrition** in human resource terminology refers to the phenomenon of the employees leaving the company.
- Employee Retention is the biggest challenge faced by HR in the modern economy. The best retention strategies are to be framed to curb the attrition.
- **Downsizing** occurs when a company permanently reduces its workforce. Employment downsizing has become a fact of working life as companies struggle to cut costs and adapt to changing market demands.
- **Manpower outsourcing** is required when a firm needs to complete a task in which they don't want to hire new employees. Outsourcing is an efficient way to save cost. Currently many information technology (IT) firms and call centers rely on outsourcing.
- **International Human Resource Management (IHRM)** can be defined as, a set of activities aimed at managing organisational human resources at international level to achieve organisational objectives and achieve competitive advantage over competitors at national and international level.
- International human resource management is the basis of success of any global multinational organisation. International HRM enhances employee's effectiveness to achieve goals of the organisation and meet the needs; to develop employees to assume more diverse tasks, assignments, face challenging situations and better understand the cultural variations across the nations.

- **Multiculturalism** is defined as the presence of people from two or more cultural backgrounds within an organisation.
- Multiculturalism is an indisputable fact of life in today's world. However, managing multiculturalism is indeed a challenge both at the, governance as well as managerial levels.
- **Cross Cultural Training (CCT)** in general can be defined as "Any intervention aimed at increasing an individual's capability to cope with work in foreign environment".
- Cross cultural training (CCT) has become an increasingly important human resource development activity due to the surge of globalisation. The need for cross-cultural capabilities has become crucial to conduct international business.

Case Study

(1) A Foreign Business Partner

When Singapore based Salton and Salton was contracted by a large conglomerate in Taiwan, the President of Salton and Salton was quite surprised. For two years, Salton and Salton had been looking for an overseas conglomerate that would be interested in building and selling its high-tech electronic equipment under a licensing agreement.

(a) The Taiwanese conglomerate has proposed Salton and Salton that the two companies enter into a joint venture type of licensing agreement. The way in which the business deal will work is the following.

The Taiwanese will set up manufacturing facilities and create a marketing group to sell Salton and Salton's high tech electronic equipment.

(b) Salton and Salton will train 50 manufacturing and so sales people from the conglomerate so that the latter understand how to make and sell this equipment. This training will take place in states.

(c) Salton and Salton will have the right to send people to the manufacturing facility to ensure that the equipment is manufactured according to the specifications and will also have the right to travel with the sales people to ensure that the equipment is being sold properly.

The arrangement sounds fine to the President of Salton and Salton. However, before he agrees to anything, he wants to get more information on how to do business with Taiwanese. If we are going to enter into a business venture with foreign company, I think, we owe it to ourselves to know something about their culture and customs. I'd like to know how to interact effectively with these people and to get an idea about the types of problems we might have in communicating with them.

Questions:

1. What type of culture related problems are there that could result in misunderstanding between the two parties?
2. If you were advising the president, what type of information would you suggest to be gathered?
3. Suggest an outline of the training programs to be conducted in this context.

(2) Virtual Working Employment

Virtual corporations are those corporations, which are open for business 24 hours of the day, every day of the year and accessible to any customer, in any part of the world, on real time basis.

The culture of urgency, combined with the freedom of setting one's own hours, makes accountability paramount in these organisations. In a much decentralised environment of the virtual company, leadership calls for great degree of visibility, both to the employees and the customers. All managers carry laptops so that they can be in constant touch with the company at large.

This twenty-four hour seven days a week culture, however eats into personal time of its managers. It is common for the employees to have conference calls during 'off hours' with some member of the team. So, during one heated development, conference calls were coordinated during a time period spanning mid-day for Pune, early morning in Japan, close to midnight in Thailand.

Questions:

1. What type of recruitment approach should be used by virtual corporation?
2. Discuss suitable compensation policies for the employees of these corporation(s).
3. Highlight various strategies to be developed by HR.

Questions For Discussion

1. What are the recent trends of motivation?
2. Does retention of employees help in building up a strong team?
3. Is attrition necessary to have a productive team?
4. Give the benefits and limitations of outsourcing man power.

5. Compare IHRM with domestic HRM.

6. What is multiculturalism?

7. Explain the term Cross Cultural Training (CCT).

8. Explain the differential approaches in HRM.

9. Define the terms HCN, PCN, TCN.

Questions From Previous Pune University Examinations

1. Discuss in detail various trends of Attrition in Modern Business World and also suggest the possible solutions. **(April - 2012)**

2. Discuss in detail various trends of Attrition and give suitable solutions for solving the problem of Attrition. **(Oct. - 2012)**

3. Discuss in detail various trends of Attrition and give suitable solutions for solving the problem of Attrition. **(April - 2013)**

UNIVERSITY QUESTION PAPER

APRIL 2015

(2013 PATTERN)

Time : 3 Hours   Max. Marks : 80

Instructions to the candidates :

1. Question No. seven is compulsory.
2. Solve any four questions from the Question No. one to six.
3. All questions carry equal marks.
4. Draw a neat diagrams wherever necessary

Q.1. Explain the development of Human Resource Management concept. Discuss in detail the role and responsibilities of Human Resource Manager.

Q.2. Explain in detail the recent trends and challenges in Human Resource Management.

Q.3. Explain in detail the concept of Manpower Planning. How does it facilitate the career planning in the organisation ?

Q.4. What is training ? Discuss in detail the various types of training methods with its advantages and disadvantages.

Q.5. Discuss the concept of Performance Appraisal with the various methods of it in detail.

Q.6. What is Attrition ? Discuss the various solutions to minimize the problem of attrition.

Q.7. Write notes on **(any four)** :

    (a) Promotion and Transfer

    (b) Job Description

    (c) Merit Rating

    (d) Cross Culture Training

    (e) Types Interviews.

www.ingramcontent.com/pod-product-compliance
Lightning Source LLC
Chambersburg PA
CBHW080052190426
43201CB00035B/2270